Exploring Outdoor Science

Hundreds of Science Activities for Teaching Children

Compiled by the Editor of Lollipops Magazine

Fearon Teacher Aids
A Division of Frank Schaffer Publications, Inc.

Senior Editor: Kristin Eclov
Editor: Donna Borst
Interior Illustration: Becky Radtke
Cover Design: Redlane Studio
Cover Illustration: F.A.B. Artists

© Fearon Teacher Aids
A Division of Frank Schaffer Publications, Inc.
23740 Hawthorne Boulevard
Torrance, CA 90505-5927

FE7951   ISBN 1-56417-951-6

2 3 4 5 6 7 8 9

Contents

To the Teacher

Exploring Outdoor Science is a compilation taken from past issues of *Lollipops* magazine, which has been in classrooms all over the world for over 18 years. After all of this time, we looked back at the wonderful material sitting on our shelves and decided it was time to share the wealth of ideas that have accumulated over the years. We sifted through 85 back issues to try and determine the best of the best, and have thus far come up with three books filled with fun, practical, and innovative material. It was a truly painstaking process to try and choose just enough material to fill these 64 pages–we were amazed at just how many exciting ideas there were to choose from. As we carefully went through every issue of *Lollipops*, we were constantly making such comments as "Wow, what a terrific idea!" and "Kids will absolutely love this!" Even those of us who have been with the magazine for many years, had forgotten some of the gems that lay between those covers. It was like finding a lost treasure of wonderful educational jewels, and we are truly excited to be able to share them with you through these books.

Lollipops continues to be one of the most creative and practical early childhood resources available, and has proven to be highly popular with teachers of children in preschool through first grade. Each issue is packed with bulletin boards, classroom decorations, recipes, crafts, stories, poems, thematic units, activities, and ideas for every subject area. Perhaps the best thing of all is that every idea, activity, and unit has been written by teachers just like you. These are people who know what works in a classroom and what doesn't. People who realize that teachers don't have all day to prepare for one lesson and who know the value of making learning fun. If you have ideas that you would like to share with other early childhood teachers through *Lollipops* magazine, we would love to hear from you. You may submit your ideas to *Lollipops*, 3427 Pheasant Run Drive, Wever, IA, 52658. If you would like to subscribe to *Lollipops*, please call 1-800-264-9873.

Other books in this series include:
> *Exploring Math: Hundreds of Math Activities for Teaching Young Children*
> *Exploring Themes: Hundreds of Activities for Teaching Themes to Young Children*

Rain

Don't save a study of rain for a rainy day. Use these activities on a sunny day or even inside the classroom to familiarize your students with the cause and effect of rain.

Creek Making

Help children understand how rainfall and earth contours help form waterways by the following experiment. Fill a sprinkling can with water (several cans, if available). Have children shake their rainfalls over various surfaces similar to the Earth: a level cement block (street), a slanted block (street on a hill), a dry level sponge, and a wet slanted sponge (all representing various conditions of the Earth's surface). Place all surfaces on a tabletop. Have kids vigorously shake water on each surface on a tabletop, noting how each surface reacts to the "rain." Ask children which type of surface is most favorable to a creek formation. Are there any other ways creeks are formed? (underground springs, running from ponds or lakes) How did rocks get into the creek?

Rain Reading

Read the book *When the Wind Stops* by Charlotte Zolotow (HarperCollins, 1997). Create a dance having children demonstrate rain, wind, snow, sun, and so on.

Rain Clouds

Have the children look out the window on a cloudy day, and ask them to describe the kinds of clouds they see. Ask if they can predict rain from the clouds today. A flat layer of clouds (stratus) usually indicates rain. High, wispy, hair-like clouds (cirrus), or puffy cumulus clouds (great for imagination play) are seen on clear days.

Point out how shade is formed when a cloud passes in front of the sun. Demonstrate how rain is formed by boiling water in a pot. The water diminishes due to evaporation. When a lid is put on the pot (similar to the dust particles within a cloud), condensation occurs, forming raindrops on the undersurface of the lid. Shake the pot lid to demonstrate rain. Children can make a rain and cloud picture by gluing cotton-ball clouds and small silver sequin raindrops on paper.

Raindrop Rings

Have the children observe raindrops as they hit a surface. Ask them to notice where each drop makes the biggest splash: on pavement, soil, or grass. Have kids watch the rings in a puddle as they are formed by raindrops. Indoors, this observation can be carried out by children shaking a very wet paintbrush over various surfaces: box of soil, a plant, or linoleum. Children may simulate the feel of rain on their skin by wetting their hands and shaking water on their classmates. Invite the children to smell the air outdoors after the rain. Then ask them to describe it.

Rainbows

Rainbow Race

Show children photographs of rainbows. Ask, "When do we see a rainbow?" "Does the rainbow last a long time?" "What are the colors of the rainbow?" Give the children a sample of each rainbow color, and have them collect natural examples of each color outdoors. Let the children arrange the nature color samples they found in the usual sequence of rainbow colors: red on top, orange, yellow, green, blue, indigo, and violet.

What Makes a Rainbow?

When rays of the sun strike falling raindrops, a colored light appears in th sky. This is a rainbow. They are curved, appearing after a storm when the su shines on still falling raindrops. Stripes of the rainbow are always red, orang yellow, green, blue, indigo, and violet.

Easy Science Experiments to Try

1. In a glass of water, place a small mirror, making sure the sun will shine o the mirror. Turn the glass until you see a rainbow reflect on a wall.
2. Using a garden hose, spray a fine mist of water, standing with your bac to the sun. A rainbow will appear in the water mist.
3. To see colors combine, make a cardboard disk coloring the three primar colors on it in equal proportions. Thread it with string and spin the dis rapidly. As the colors combine, the disk will appear white; then as the dis slows down, the colors return.

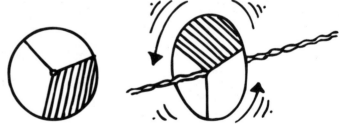

4. Play with a store-bought prism. It will separate colors as you hold it int the light.

6

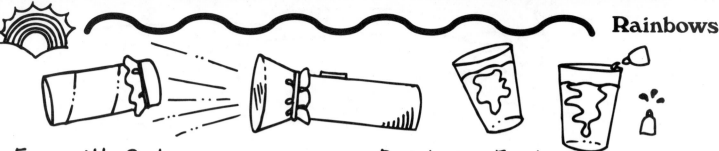

Fun with Colors

The sense of sight is wonderful to explore. Here are some examples of fun with colors.

1. Place colored cellophane over the ends of toilet-paper tubes, using rubber bands to secure. Colored cellophane can be bought in craft stores. The world looks different in so many colors.

2. You can also place colored cellophane over flashlights—fun in the dark!

3. Put food coloring in water using baby food jars. Start with primary colors (red, yellow, and blue). Experiment mixing colors to obtain secondary hues: orange, green, and purple.
   red and yellow = orange
   yellow and blue = green
   red and blue = purple

Rainbow Explosion

Materials

- cake pan
- powdered milk
- water
- different food colorings
- liquid detergent

Procedure

Cover bottom of pan with 1" (2.5 cm) of powdered milk. Add water to cover, being careful not to mix. Put several drops of food colorings on top. Observe rainbow shadings. Squeeze a few drops of detergent on top. Observe as the oil in the detergent causes colors to explode and merge.

Rainbow Toast

Materials

- white bread slices
- milk
- food coloring (spectrum colors)
- containers for food coloring
- paintbrushes
- toaster

Procedure

Put several tablespoons (30 ml) of milk into each container. Have the children help you add food coloring to the milk to make rainbow colors (red, orange, yellow, green, blue, indigo, violet). Paint rainbows on the white bread slices using the milk paint. Be careful not to let the bread get soaked with milk. Toast bread in a toaster set at light toast. Spread your toast with whipped cream cheese tinted in rainbow colors.

Puddles

If it's springtime, puddles are plentiful. Why not spark your spring sense program? Play with puddles offers young children fun and fantastic ways to solve some special problems and puzzles. Puddles are a pretty and provocative natural phenomenon. They provide endless possibilities to explore, enjoy, and learn. Puddles can also help young children pacify their abounding curiosity and gradually build their understanding of scientific concepts.

Puddles are often a spontaneously formed material and can disappear almost like magic. So—plan ahead. Be prepared with plenty of perky puddle pointers.

Peek and Poke

After several rainy days, a night of downpour rain, or a quickie springtime shower, look out the playground window with a small group of children. Have them observe the appearance of the playground. Be enthusiastic. Possible points to discuss:

1. Where do puddles come from?
2. Why are there so many? So few?
3. Why do we see puddles of different shapes? Different sizes?
4. What visitors might come to the puddles?
5. What can we do with puddles?

Group discussions are helpful in assessing the children's thinking levels and in assisting appropriate planning. Record responses on a chart or tape recorder.

Story Writing

Draw or paint a picture of the playground. Show puddles and then tell a story.

Where Does a Puddle Go?

You will need two small jars or dishes, each half filled with water. Cover one dish and leave one exposed. Watch to see what happens. Record your observations over several days.

The Ripple Effect

After tossing pebbles in puddles and observing the ripple effect, try this.

1. Arrange a set of six concentric paper circles in order with largest on bottom.
2. Use a crayon to draw a series of rings from smallest to largest. The circles should look like the ripples in a puddle of water.

8

Plan a Puddle Walk

Pursue the interest in puddles or promote it by going on a puddle walk in your playground area or the school neighborhood. Possible points to discuss:

1. What special clothing do we need?
2. Why are bright colors useful on puddle days?
3. Why are boots or rubbers necessary?
4. Why is it important to be sensible and safe?
5. Why is it fun, or not fun, to walk through a puddle? Jump in? Jump over?
6. How does your mother feel when you want to play in puddles?
7. How will going on a puddle walk be helpful to us?

Looking for Clues

Place a marker (chalk, tape, flag) beside several puddle areas. When the puddle dries, examine the spot for clues as to how and why the puddles formed in that particular spot.

Measure Around and Across

Scissors, string, or yarn will be necessary. Measure the size of several puddles—around and across. Compare the sizes.

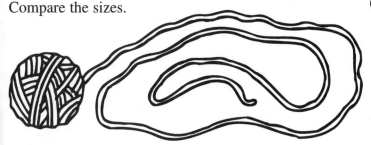

Be a Puddle Detective

Look in one puddle. What can you see? Touch? Smell? Hear? Make a list of all the objects you see in the puddle. Use a magnifying glass to help.

Scoop Up the Treasure

Collect as many objects as possible from the puddle. Place them in a container and return to the classroom. On a tray, sort the puddle treasures into natural or man-made categories. Arrange them on cardboard and glue in place. Label: *Our Puddle Treasures.*

Follow the Leader

Choose a leader. Walk, hop, skip, and jump around a path of puddles in the playground area.

Play Games

One child alone or two together may play by . . .
- sailing a small boat.
- pulling a pebble attached to a string.
- floating pieces of paper (manilla, typing, napkin, cardboard).
- sinking five objects.
- making reflections and mirror images.

Gardens

Introduce your class to gardening and cultivate a love of the Earth while learning about nature, food production, and plant growth. Gardening aids the development of motor skills and offers a hands-on approach to sequencing. Watching plants grow and flourish promotes a sense of accomplishment and enhances self-esteem.

Seeds Are Food

Bring in a variety of nuts in shells, as well as sunflower and pumpkin seeds, as examples of seeds we can eat. Open several nuts and examine the nut meats. Allow the children to sample the seeds. Have the children help prepare an edible-seeds display for your science area by gluing a sample of each seed onto a cardboard chart. Label each seed. **Note:** Be sure to find out if any children have food allergies and be aware that seeds can be a choking hazard.

Seeds Grow Food

Share several seed packets with the class, include flower, vegetable, and fruit seeds. Talk about the pictures on the fronts of the seed packets, naming each plant and deciding which ones we eat. Classify the packets by category. Open several seed packets and note the differences in the seeds. Next, cover a bulletin board or door with white paper and add a long, green paper streamer to make a vine. Add large green paper leaves. Have the children search magazines for pictures of foods we get from plants. Place a food picture on each leaf.

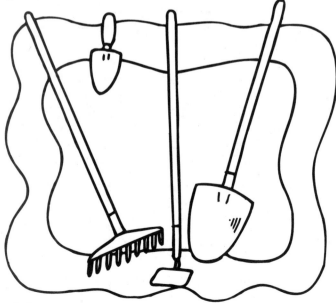

Tools of the Trade

Bring in examples of gardening tools, such as a spade, hoe, rake, shovel, trowel, watering can, and pail. Name each tool and discuss its use. Provide a place for the children to experiment with the tools (sandbox or outdoor gardening spot).

Discovering Seeds

Provide samples of real fruit, vegetables, and flowers. Name each item and have the children help locate the seeds in each. Save some of each kind of seed to plant at a later date.

Acting the Part

Have the children dramatize the gardening process with the following song.

The Happy Gardener

(To the tune of "Here We Go 'Round the Mulberry Bush")
This is the way we dig the holes,
dig the holes, dig the holes.
This is the way we dig the holes,
in our springtime garden.

Additional Verses

1. This is the way we plant the seeds.
2. This is the way we rake the soil.
3. This is the way we water the plants.
4. This is the way we pull the weeds.

Plant Growth

Help your class discover what a plant needs to grow. Let them plant seeds in three different cups. After the seedlings sprout and begin to develop, have the class conduct a plant experiment. Provide one plant with water and light, the second plant with water but no light, and the third plant with light but no water. Observe the plants after two or more days and compare their growth. When the plants without light or water begin to fail, resume proper plant treatment and attempt to revive each to normal growth.

Garden Graph

Set out magazines, gardening catalogs, scissors, and glue. Ask for the children's assistance in cutting out pictures of fruits, vegetables, and flowers. Set up a bar graph to sort the pictures by color or category. Invite the children to glue their cut-outs to the graph in appropriate places. Ask them to name and talk about the pictures they cut out.

Flower Puzzle

Provide the children with real flowers, scissors, paper, and glue. Name the parts of a flower and discuss the job of each part. Help the children cut their flowers apart so they will have a blossom, stem, leaves, and roots (if your flowers include roots). Then have them glue the flower "puzzle" pieces onto the paper in their proper places, forming a complete flower.

Just Imagine

Another activity to spark children's imaginations, as well as to help them express their knowledge of plant life, is to have them imagine what life would be like as a plant. Give each child a paper with the title *My Life as a Plant* written at the top. Ask each child to draw a picture of his or her favorite plant. Then have children write or dictate a few sentences about what they think life would be like as that plant.

Up Close

Share the following rhyme with the children, then discuss what they think they would find if they were tiny enough to walk among the plants in a garden. How would the plants look, feel, and smell? What else might they see? (insects, worms) How would these things appear? Afterward, provide children with magnifying glasses and let them examine different plants, soil, and rocks.

More Seeds

Plan a visit to a local garden center. The children will be able to experience firsthand all of the kinds of materials available for garden use. Take note of the tools, fertilizers, seeds, and so on. Ask if children can name any of the plants present. Purchase some seeds to plant at school.

Jar Garden

Sprout your own alfalfa seeds to harvest and eat. First, soak the alfalfa seeds in water overnight and drain. Place the seeds in a mayonnaise jar, filling about one third of the jar. Cover the jar with cheesecloth and secure with a rubber band. Store at room temperature. Rinse once or twice daily by filling the jar with water and emptying through the cheesecloth. The sprouts should be ready to harvest in about four or five days, when they are green. Invite the children to try a sprout sandwich by adding wheat bread and mayonnaise to the harvest.

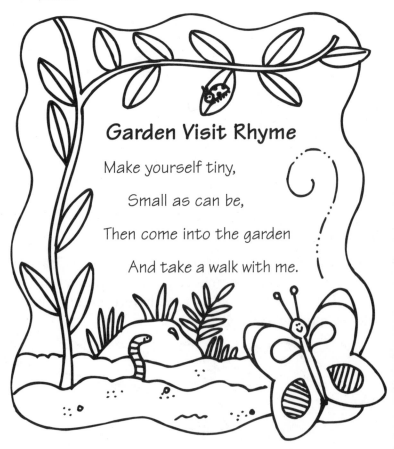

Garden Visit Rhyme

Make yourself tiny,

Small as can be,

Then come into the garden

And take a walk with me.

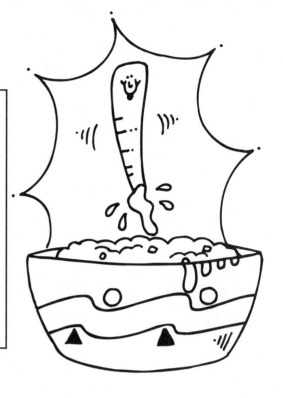

Garden Snack

Have the children wash and slice a variety of fresh vegetables. Let them help prepare the following recipe, then dip as desired.

Vegetable Dip

2/3 cup (160 ml) mayonnaise   1 Tbsp. (15 ml) onion, chopped
2/3 cup (160 ml) sour cream   1 tsp. (5 ml) dillweed
1 Tbsp. (15 ml) parsley

Combine all ingredients and blend well.

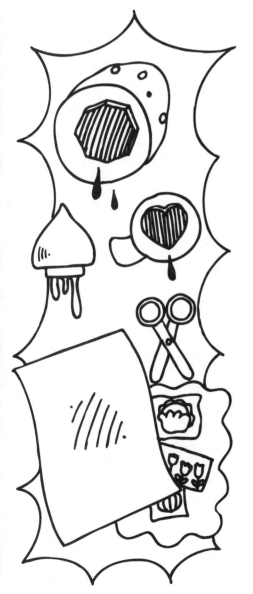

Garden Shapes

Allow children to experiment with different shapes and textures by using paint and food products. Make stamps by cutting cross-sections of various fruits and vegetables (potatoes, peppers, mushrooms, celery, and so on). Have them dip the food stamps into the paint and stamp the shapes onto paper. They may want to label some of their designs when the paint dries.

Garden Patch

Provide brown paper, magazines, scissors, and glue. Have the children cut any desired shape from the brown paper to be their garden patch. Invite them to cut out magazine pictures of things they would like to grow in their gardens and then glue these pictures to the paper.

Counting Seeds

Have the children use real seeds to plant a pretend garden on the "Planting Seeds" sheet (page 14). Have them read the number on the seed packet by each row; then glue the same number of seeds in that row.

A Garden of My Own

Provide seeds, soil, and containers for the children to start their own dish gardens. When the seedlings begin to grow, encourage the children to take their plants home to replant, care for, and harvest.

Planting Seeds

Glue the correct number of seeds in each row.

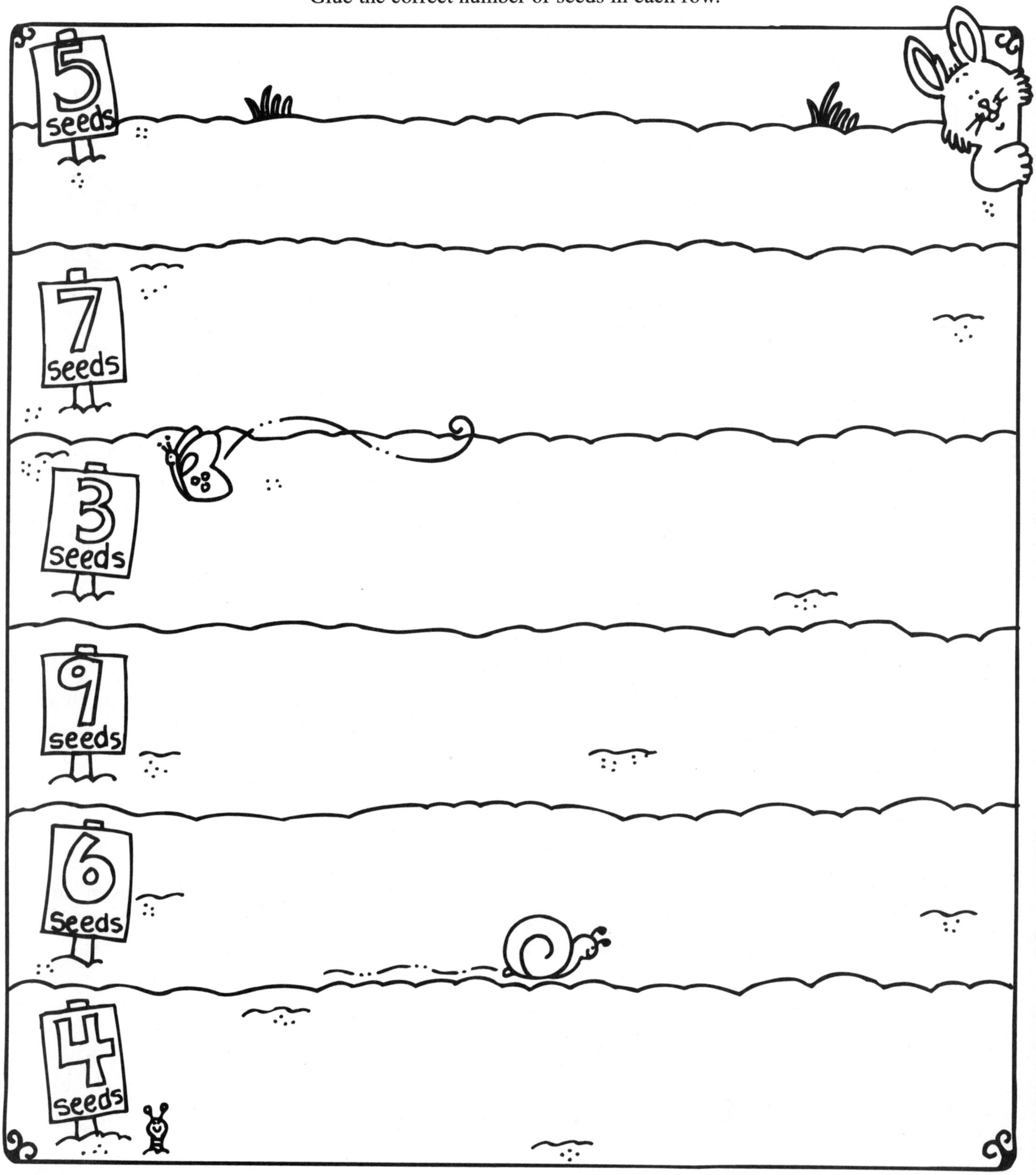

5 seeds

7 seeds

3 seeds

9 seeds

6 seeds

4 seeds

Reproducible

Wind

Ask children to share what they know about wind. What is it? Can you hear it, see it, taste it, smell it, touch it? How does the wind help us? Then have children take turns making wind sounds. Have them create their own small winds by blowing or waving their hands. Make a list of ways in which we use the wind.

Windmill Arms

Have the children pretend to be windmills by moving their arms in a circular motion. Ask them to make small, large, and giant circles. Have them move both arms in a clockwise motion and then a counterclockwise motion. Ask them to move both arms in the same direction and then in opposite directions. Have them be very slow-moving windmills and then change to swift windmills.

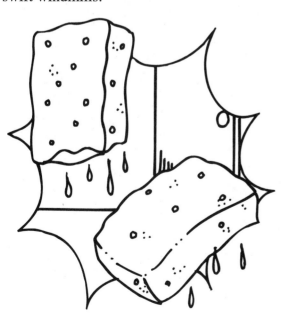

Rub a Dub, Dub

For this sailing activity, each child will need a small margarine container, a piece of modeling clay, a craft stick, crayons, scissors, and tape. Ask each child to design and cut out a sail from paper. Tape the sail to the top of the craft stick. Press the clay firmly into the margarine container and then push the bottom of the craft stick into the clay. Provide children with a water table or basin in which to sail their boats. Who will make the wind?

Wet Rag Experiment

On a windy day, invite your class to join you in a wind experiment. Wet two identical cloths or sponges. Find places to hang one indoors and one outdoors. Ask the children to hypothesize which one will dry first. Periodically, have different students check on both items. Which was first to dry? Ask the children why they think this happened.

Balloon Races

Supervise the children in balloon-blowing races. Have two children get on their hands and knees at the starting line. Place a balloon on the floor in front of each child. The object is to crawl along the floor and keep blowing on the balloon until it crosses the finish line.

Ping-Pong™ Drop

Have the children work in pairs at opposite sides of a table. One child will blow on a Ping-Pong™ ball to move it across the table. The second child will catch the ball as it drops off the side of the table and then take his or her turn blowing the ball back to the first child.

Musical Wind

Ask the students to name things that are moved by wind. Help them to remember seeds, sailboats, clothes on the line, clouds, and tree branches. Can they add to the list? Have them pretend to be one of these objects on a windy day. As they bend, stretch, and sway, play different types of music. Have them match their wind movements to the music. What kind of wind does soft, slow music remind them of? How would the wind blow if the music was loud and fast?

Tossing It to the Wind

Place several objects in two boxes and have the children sort them into two categories: light and heavy. Objects could include cotton balls, beads, feathers, erasers, straws, paper, balls, leaves, grapes, and yarn.

Once the children have sorted the objects, go outside on a windy day. Make a circle of children. Have children take turns in the center with the two boxes. The child in the center with the two boxes chooses one object and tosses it up in the wind. All the children watch what happens. The teacher records what happens to each object in either pictures or simple words.

Back in the classroom, the teacher places the boxes of objects and the recorded responses in a science/writing center. Children are encouraged to record what happened in their wind experiment.

The Wind and the Seeds

The tiny seed is carried by the wind to a place far-away to grow. Go on a seed hunt. Find the seeds that the wind will carry to other places. Toss them up and watch them travel. (After the activity, gather the seeds and put them all in a plastic see-through bag. Toss them in a trash can after the day's seed trip.)

The Wild Wind

The wind can be calm or wild. In the past few years, young children have been terrified by the destruction that winds and tornadoes have caused. In some parts of the country, the wind blowing is a sure sign of a storm. In other parts of the country, the wind seems to blow all the time.

Many times these sensitive issues are better dealt with ahead of time to desensitize children and prepare them for what might happen. Four books do just that. *Tornado Alert* (Harper & Row, 1988) and *Hurricane Watch* (Harper & Row, 1988) present factual information with pictures about the storms. Safety standards are included. *Storm in the Night* (Harper & Row, 1988) and *Hurricane* (Clarion Books, 1990) tell about families weathering storms. Both books are good ones to begin conversations with children about what they should do in case of a storm.

Children's Books

Branley, F. M. *Tornado Alert.* (Harper & Row, 1988).
   A *Let's Read and Find Out Book* with pictures and facts about tornadoes. Another in the series is *Hurricane Watch.*
Stolz, M. *Storm in the Night.* (Harper & Row, 1988).
   In the dark, an African American grandfather, boy, and cat share stories and listen to the noises of the city during a storm.
Wiesner, D. *Hurricane.* (Clarion Books, 1990).
   Two young boys weather the hurricane with their family. During the days afterwards, they imagine that the old, felled elm tree is a pirate ship, a private place, a spaceship, and the jungle.
Ets, M.H. *Gilberto and the Wind.* (Viking Press, 1963).
Carle, E. *The Tiny Seed.* (Scholastic Inc., 1987).

The Sun

Science with the Sun

Introduce the science concepts of the sun, such as light, heat, dehydration, evaporation, and liquid and solid states. Ask them what whey think is the most important thing in our world or our universe. The sun! Have children suggest ways the sun is important. Without the sun, the Earth would be a dark, frozen, dead planet. There would be no light, no warmth, wind, or rain. There would be no plants, no animals, and no people. Nothing can live without the sun.

Sun Prints

Demonstrate the power of the sun by helping your students make sun-print pictures. Use items from nature (rocks, leaves, grass, bark) or items from around the classroom (pencils, keys, paper clips).

Choose a sunny location. Arrange items on dark-colored paper and place in a sunny location. Begin the project early in the day to give the sun plenty of time to do its work. When the papers have faded, collect all of the objects used for sun prints and place in containers. Help students find the real objects and match them to the sun prints on the paper.

Sun Clocks

Before mechanical clocks were invented, sundials were used for telling time. A special pointer, called a *gnomon*, casts a shadow on a circular object. The shadow marks the hours and moves as the sun moves across the sky.

Have your students make shadow clocks with their bodies and then make simple sundials to take home.

Shadow Clocks

Two children can work together. One child stands in a place in the yard where the sun will be shining all day. Have the other child trace the shadow of his partner. Every two hours after that, have the child stand with his feet in the same place and have his shadow drawn again. Write the time above the shadow each time. At the end of the day the children will see that the positions and shapes of their shadows have changed.

18

Melting Magic

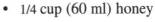

Use ice in many forms to help the children understand concepts of liquid and solid. Fill empty milk cartons with water leaving some room for expansion and place in freezer. Remove from the freezer when solid and run under hot water just enough to make cracks in the ice. Peel the carton away and set ice in a pan. Chip several small holes in the ice and place several drops of food coloring in the holes. Set pan in the sun and watch the ice return to a liquid state. Talk about the colors that appear as the ice melts.

Frozen Fingers
Materials
- 1 square of aluminum foil per student

Have each student place one hand in the middle of his or her sheet of foil with fingers spread. The student should use the other hand to reach under the foil to push foil around the fingers and hand. Mold the foil to make a dish shaped just like the student's hand. Fill the dish with water. Freeze and carefully peel off the foil. Set in the sun and see whose hand melts first. (For a special treat, fill with juice and eat the frozen fingers for a snack.)

Sunshine Candy: Fruit Leather

Take advantage of the summer's fruit surplus and give your children the opportunity to learn about dehydration. Your students will learn that the sun can remove water from fruit and produce a wonderful "sun" candy that tastes great and is still good for them. This recipe is easy to make.

Ingredients

- 4 cups (.95 l) fruit
- 1/4 cup (60 ml) honey

Clean fruit and puree it in a blender with honey. Stir together until blended. Pour in a saucepan and heat to almost boiling. Cool. Pour puree 1/4" (.625 cm) thick onto trays or baking sheets lined with plastic wrap. Place trays outside for one or two days. Trays can be covered with cheesecloth to protect the fruit mixture from insects. The cheesecloth should not touch the fruit mixture.

The fruit mixture will begin to get pliable, and it is ready when you can peel it from the plastic wrap. Remove the "leather" from the plastic while it is still warm and roll it up. Wrap it in plastic wrap.

Note: The following fruits need to be heated to retain color and prevent darkening: fresh peaches, pears, apples, apricots, cherries, and nectarines. No cooking is required when using fresh plums, raspberries, blackberries, and boysenberries.

Sundials and Shadows

Did you know that the sun is our oldest known clock? Hundreds of years ago, people told time by the sun. They created clocks known as sundials to record the time. The sundial was first used in Babylon as early as 2000 B.C. A sundial indicates the time by measuring the angle of a shadow cast by the sun. People used such clocks for almost 3500 years. (Clocks as we know them were not invented until about 1400 A.D.)

Children can make their own sundials with a paper plate, a piece of clay, and a pencil or slender stick. Use the clay to attach the pencil to the center of the paper plate. Take the plate outside at eight o'clock in the morning on a sunny, windless day. Secure the plate to the ground. Trace the outline of the pencil's shadow on the paper plate and write the time on it. Do this each hour throughout the day. Notice that some shadows are longer than others and that the shortest shadow is at noon. When your sundial is finished, you can use it to tell time. Make sure your noon shadow always points to the north.

Seeing Light

Most of the time we can't actually see the light from the sun, yet we know it's there. There are several activities students can do to see light beams. In a dark room, clap a chalkboard eraser in a beam of light from a flashlight or slide projector. The light reflects off the chalk particles, enabling us to see the light beam. The same thing happens in nature. If there is dust or other particles in the air, we can sometimes see the beams of light from the sun.

Another activity children enjoy requires a glass of water, a few drops of milk, a flashlight, and an index card. Cut a narrow rectangular hole in the center of the card. Stir a few drops of milk into the water in the glass and place the card on top of it. Hold a flashlight about a foot (30 cm) away, and shine the light through the hole. The light shines on the tiny drops of milk, making the light beam visible in the glass.

Another activity to try requires a pair of binoculars and a sheet of paper. Hold the binoculars so that the sun shines through one of the lenses. Move the paper around until you get an image of the sun on the sheet of paper.

Sunlight and Day and Night

Ask the children how the sun is responsible for day and night. Does the sun really set at night and rise in the morning? To help children understand how the sun gives us day and night, use a globe to represent the Earth and a desk lamp to represent the sun. Place the globe about two feet (60 cm) away from the lamp in a darkened room. What happens to the globe when the lamp is lit? Half of the Earth is in daylight, and the other half is in darkness (night). Have a child mark an X with chalk on your state. Then slowly spin the globe from west to east. What happens to your state? Notice how it goes from daylight to night to daylight again as the Earth turns. Also notice that the east receives the sun's light before the west does. Be sure the children understand that it is the Earth, not the sun, that is moving. The sun does not really set or rise, although it appears to.

Ask the children where most of our light comes from at night. Children will probably respond that the moon gives us our light. Actually it is the sun that is still responsible for our light. The moon does not produce light. It only reflects the light from the sun. To demonstrate this, hold a small mirror on the dark side of the globe so that light from the lamp strikes the mirror and reflects to the globe. (The mirror represents the moon.) Ask the children where the moonlight is coming from. Then ask them what will happen if we turn off the "sun." Turn off the lamp. Is there still any light coming from the "moon" (mirror)?

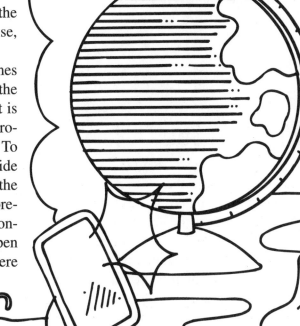

Invisible Light

In addition to the colors we are able to see in the spectrum, sunlight contains other kinds of light that are invisible. One of these is infrared light. Infrared light is used for radiation therapy and photography. The other invisible light is ultraviolet light. Ultraviolet rays help our bodies to produce vitamin D, but too much ultraviolet light can be harmful. Ultraviolet light can cause sunburn and damage our eyes. Emphasize that it is important to avoid looking directly at the sun or to spend too much time in the sun (especially in the summer).

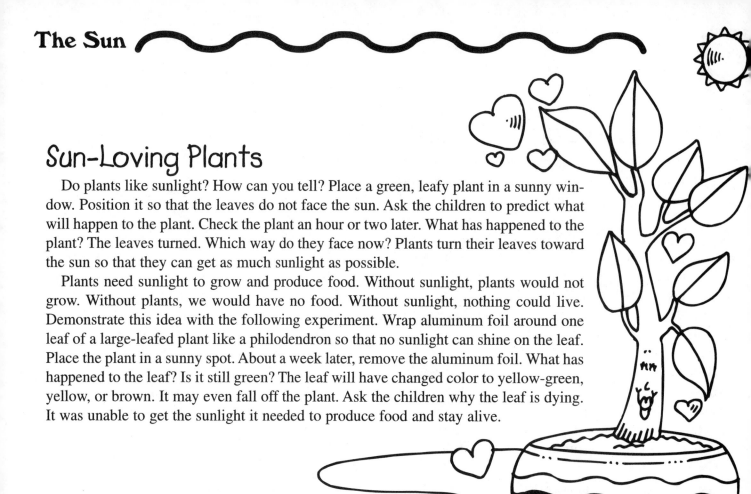

Sun-Loving Plants

Do plants like sunlight? How can you tell? Place a green, leafy plant in a sunny window. Position it so that the leaves do not face the sun. Ask the children to predict what will happen to the plant. Check the plant an hour or two later. What has happened to the plant? The leaves turned. Which way do they face now? Plants turn their leaves toward the sun so that they can get as much sunlight as possible.

Plants need sunlight to grow and produce food. Without sunlight, plants would not grow. Without plants, we would have no food. Without sunlight, nothing could live. Demonstrate this idea with the following experiment. Wrap aluminum foil around one leaf of a large-leafed plant like a philodendron so that no sunlight can shine on the leaf. Place the plant in a sunny spot. About a week later, remove the aluminum foil. What has happened to the leaf? Is it still green? The leaf will have changed color to yellow-green, yellow, or brown. It may even fall off the plant. Ask the children why the leaf is dying. It was unable to get the sunlight it needed to produce food and stay alive.

How Do We See Color?

Introduce the words *reflect* and *reflection,* and have the children pronounce them. Ask the children if any of them have reflectors on their bicycles. What do these reflectors do? When we say that something reflects light, we mean that the light bounces back. Light behaves like a ball kicked against a wall. It bounces back. Use a ball to demonstrate this idea.

If things did not reflect light, we would not be able to see them. In order for us to see something, two things must happen: 1) light must shine on the object and 2) the light must reflect (bounce) off the object to our eyes. Ask the children why it is difficult to see things in a dark room or at night.

Some things reflect little light, while others reflect a lot of light. A mirror or a shiny metal surface reflects nearly all the light. Most things, however, reflect only a part of the spectrum and keep back the rest of it. Different objects reflect back different parts of the spectrum. The part that bounces back to our eyes is the color of the object. Help the children to realize that when light shines on an object, all the colors in the light are shining on it. For example, when sunlight shines on the grass, the colors red, orange, yellow, green, blue, indigo, and violet are shining on it. The grass keeps back all the colors except green, and the green part of the light is reflected back to our eyes. Objects that are white reflect all the colors. Objects that are black reflect none of the colors.

Cut out a variety of pictures of objects that are primarily one color: an apple, blue jeans, an evergreen tree, a snowman, an orange, a banana, grapes, and so on. Glue each picture to a separate sheet of paper which is attached to a stack of paper strips, each paper strip is divided into six squares. Ask the children to look at each object and color one or more squares to show the parts of the light that each object reflects. After checking a child's color, tear off the top strip and the picture is ready for another child's use. If you are using objects that are white (example: a snowman), check to be sure the child has colored all six squares a different color to show that white reflects all the colors.

Solar Energy

Besides light energy, the sun also produces heat energy. Often we refer to this type of energy as solar energy. Try some of the following experiments with the children to demonstrate the sun's heat energy.

Ask the children if things get warmer in the sunlight than they do in the shade. How much warmer? Pour equal amounts of very cold water into two Styrofoam™ cups. Place a thermometer in each cup and record the temperature. Place one cup in the shade and the other in direct sunlight. Check the temperature of each cup after five, ten, and fifteen minutes. Have the children make a simple graph to show the temperature changes in the water. Use one color for shade and another for sunlight.

Children might also enjoy experimenting to see which color absorbs the sun's heat the most. Place six sheets of different colored construction paper (red, yellow, blue, green, white, and black) in sunlight. Place an ice cube of uniform size on each. Which ice cube melts first? Which ice cube melts last? Which colors get the warmest? What color clothes would be the coolest to wear in the summer? Why do people paint solar energy collectors black?

Solar energy can also be used to cook food. Have the children try baking small pieces of food (example: apple or hot dog) in a simple solar cooker. Place a piece of apple or hot dog in a clear plastic glass. Wrap the glass securely in clear plastic wrap. Tape a piece of black paper around the glass. Then wrap a piece of paper toweling around the sides and bottom of the glass over the black paper. Place this glass inside another clear plastic glass. Finally, wrap a sheet of aluminum foil, shiny side in, around the outside glass to form a cone shape as shown in the diagram. Place the solar cooker in direct sunlight so that the sun shines into the top of the cone. Allow your food to cook for about an hour before eating it. Children can check to see how their food is cooking by looking down through the cone.

Shadows

Young children can oftentimes be quite alarmed when they first realize that their shadow is following them. In an attempt to run from it, they realize that they cannot. The fear is sometimes overwhelming. Even as the adult picks up the child, the shadow is still there. A basic classroom experiment with light, dark, and shadows can help children learn that shadows are a natural part of nature, occurring when light is blocked.

Shadows do occur when the light is blocked from reaching a final point. The sun shines on a person, blocking the light from shining on the pavement, wall, or other structure. The shadow shows the absence of light in that spot, forming a shape similar to the person blocking the light. The shape changes depending on the angle of the sun. The same holds true for shadows from artificial light sources. Children can see shadows of their hands if they hold them above their tables. The light from the ceiling or windows is blocked by the hand forming a shadow. The shadow changes form or size as the hand is moved closer or farther from the light source.

Shadow Cut-Outs

Materials

overhead projector, objects, paper, tape, pencils, scissors

Directions

Place an overhead projector near a chalkboard. Turn on the projector. Locate the light on the board. Tape a large piece of paper on the board. When children place objects on the overhead projector, they will be projected in a shadow on the paper. Have them vary the size of the object by moving the projector. When they have decided on a size, have them trace around the shadow and cut it out. (It's a great way to make gigantic dinosaurs!)

Shadow Silhouettes

Project the silhouette of a child on a piece of paper using a film or filmstrip projector. Cut silhouette out. Glue to a piece of contrasting paper.

Can You Believe It?

Materials

gooseneck light, paper, pencils, scissors

Directions

Place the materials on a small table and have children work in pairs. Turn on the light and bend the light to shine on the tabletop. Put a piece of paper on the table. Have each child place his or her hand between the light and the table. While one child holds his or her hand in the light, have another one trace the shadow. Challenge them to make shadows of various sizes. When they are done, glue the hands in order from largest to smallest on a long piece of paper.

Where's My Shadow?

Materials

several objects, black paper, pencils, scissors

Directions

Ask children to trace objects with a pencil onto black paper. Young children can do this best in pairs. After the object is traced, have them cut it out and place it in a box which you have entitled "Where's My Shadow?" (For preschoolers, you may have to make the "shadows" ahead of time.)

After a couple of days, have children work in small groups to find the shadow that matches the object, place the objects on a piece of paper with double-sided tape to suggest that the black shape is the shadow.

Night and Day

After demonstrating night and day using a globe and flashlight, place the globe, a flashlight, the chart with day and night columns, and a pencil in a learning center. Have children work in small groups. One child shines the flashlight on a country on the globe. A second child records the name of the country in the "Day" column. A third child examines the night side of the globe and tells the recorder to record the night country in the "Night" column. Rotate places and have the children locate as many day and night pairs as they can.

Making Shadows

Materials

construction-paper shapes, white paper, glue, 1" (2.5 cm) sections of toilet-paper rolls, light source

Directions

Have the children cut several shapes out of construction paper. Glue them onto a toilet-paper roll. Glue the other end of the toilet-paper roll onto a piece of white paper. The construction-paper shape will make a shadow on the white paper when held in a light source.

What Could It Be?

Materials

paper, black tempera, spoon, ruler

Directions

Demonstrate to the children how to make a bloom that looks like a shadow. Fold the paper in half. Open the paper and drop one spoonful of black tempera in the center. Close the paper and rub from top to bottom with a ruler. Open the paper and let dry. Have the children write about what they think made this shadow. Children can make several flowers, trying each time to make them the exact same way. See if the flowers come out the same each time.

My Very
Own 10o'clock
Shadow
Book
by Traci

The 10 O'clock Shadow

Give each child pieces of paper and black crayons. Take a trip outside on a sunny day—at 10 a.m. or 2 p.m. might be best. Have them locate an object with a shadow. Place the paper near the object and trace the shadow on the paper. Record what the object is on the back of the paper in small print. Let the children do this as many times as they wish to make *My Very Own 10 O'clock Shadow Book*.

Predicting the Weather

For years people have tried predicting the weather. One way to determine the length of winter weather past February 2 is to see if the groundhog sees its shadow on that day. If the shadow can be seen, wintry weather will continue for about another six weeks. If it cannot be seen, wintry weather is over shortly. On February 2, cut out a groundhog shape. Take it outside at 10 o'clock in the morning. See if you can see a shadow. If the clouds are making a shadow, then no shadow will be present. If the sun is shining on a cloudless day, shadows will appear.

Keep close track of the weather for the next six weeks to see if your prediction is right. Weather is one of those things that even experts with scientific instruments and computers can follow and label but cannot predict. Older children can do this individually and record weather on an individual blank calendar.

All Day Shadows

Place several small objects outside along a sidewalk where they will not be disturbed during the day. Place the objects far enough apart that children can sit in front of the object to make a shadow drawing several times during the day and will not disturb the person next to them.

Give children different colors of colored chalk to trace the shadow onto the sidewalk several times during the day. Examine the different shapes, and sizes of the shadows. On another day, stick (with double-sided tape or playdough) the object on a piece of paper. Trace the object in different colors at various times during the day. Record the time in the upper left-hand corner of the paper with the color used at that time.

Shadows I Know

Provide children with a blank book of paper that is covered with black construction paper. On each page of the book have children draw a picture of something and its shadow—attached at the bottom of the object. A brief explanation of each shadow can be written by those children who can.

Sunny Day Challenge

Challenge the children to do these tasks with their shadows:

- Make your shadow follow you.
- Walk along following your shadow.
- Make your shadow walk along your right or left side.
- What happens to your shadow if you carry a stick?
- Make your shadows hold hands; touch head-to-head; touch in three places, in two places, in four places.

As a group, have the class do these tasks:

- Line up your shadows from smallest to largest.
- Can you make the heads of your shadows all touch a straight line?
- Line up making your shadows hold hands.

Children's Stories and Books

Aesop. "The Dog and His Shadow." In Tomie dePaola's (Ed. & Artist), *Favorite Nursery Tales* (p. 63). G.P. Putnam's Sons 1986.

Asch. F. *Bear Shadow*. Scholastic Inc., 1982.

Brown, M. *Shadow*. Macmillan Publishing Company, 1982.

Bulla. C. *What Makes a Shadow?* Thomas Y. Crowell Company, 1962.

Charlie. R. *Mother, Mother, I Feel Sick: Send for the Doctor Quick, Quick, Quick!* Parents' Magazine Press, 1966.

DePaola, T. *Favorite Nursery Tales*. G.P. Putnam's Sons, 1986.

Fleischman, P. *Shadow Play*. Harper & Row, 1990.

Goor, R, and N. Goor. *Shadows: Here, There, and Everywhere*. Alfred A. Knopf, 1981.

Simon, S. *Let's Try-It-Out: Light and Dark*. McGraw-Hill Book Company, 1970.

Stephenson, R.L. *A Child's Garden of Verses*. Random House, 1978.

Yolen, J. *Owl Moon*. Philomel Books, 1987.

Poems

Hillert, M. "Hide-and-Seek Shadow." In J. Prelutsky (Ed.), *Read-Aloud Rhymes for the Very Young* (p.25). Alfred A. Knopf, 1986.

Orleans, I. "Poor Shadow." In J. Prelutsky (Ed.), *Read-Aloud Rhymes for the Very Young* (p. 25). Alfred A. Knopf, 1986.

Stephenson, R.L. "My Shadow." In Tomie dePaola's (Ed. and Artist), *Favorite Nursery Tales* (pp. 40-41). G.P. Putnam's Sons, 1986.

Seuss, Dr. *The Shape of Me and Other Stuff*. Random House, 1973.

Silverstein, S. "Shadow Wash." In *Where the Sidewalk Ends* (p. 113). Harper & Row, 1974.

Shadows Appear in the Illustrations of These Children's Books

Brown, R. *A Dark Dark Tale*. Dial Books, 1981.

Martin, Jr. B., and Archambault. J. *Knots on a Counting Rope*. The Trumpet Club, 1987.

Greenfield, E. *Grandpa's Face*. Philomel Books, 1988.

Activities on Shadows

Courson, D. *Focus on the Arts and Science*. Good Apple, 1993.

Snow

It's winter! Fresh snow covers the ground. Celebrate the season with these science activities that teach kids about snow and foster environmental awareness.

What Is Snow?

Snow is formed when the water vapor in clouds freezes. Each snowflake is formed when thousands of water vapor droplets cling to a speck of dust or ice and freeze. The size and shape of each snowflake depends on the temperature of the clouds, how high the clouds are, and how much moisture is in them.

In general, there are three main kinds of snow. Wet snow, which contains large flakes and a lot of moisture, is heavy, packs easily, and settles on the ground with little air between the flakes. Dry, fluffy snow falls quietly, clings together, and piles up in feathery cushions with a lot of air between the flakes. Dry, powdery snow, which falls only in very cold weather, consists of tiny, light flakes that resemble flour and do not cling together.

Classifying Snowflakes

While you will never find two snowflakes that are exactly alike, all snowflakes fit into one of seven basic groups. Of these, three kinds are seen most often: stellar, plate, and plate with extensions. Catch some snowflakes and make drawings of them. Compare your snowflake drawings to the ones below. Which shape is each most like? As a class, make a bar graph showing how many of each shape were collected. Did you find snowflakes that weren't like any of these three? How were they different?

Forecast a Snowstorm

Children can make a simple device that uses air pressure to predict the weather. Stretch a piece of broken balloon tightly across the mouth of a jar and secure it with a rubber band. Put a drop of glue on the middle of the stretched balloon and place one end of a straw on the glue as shown in the diagram. Using an identical jar, attach a ruler to the jar with a rubber band. Place the jars as shown above, and note the number the straw points to on the ruler. Check the straw every few hours to see if it is changing direction. If the straw moves upward, pointing to a higher number on the ruler, the weather is likely to be warmer and clear. If the straw points downward to a lower number, snow is likely.

Catch Some Snowflakes

An hour or so before you go outside, place a piece of black felt or dark cardboard in the freezer so it becomes very cold. Take the felt or cardboard outside and catch a few snowflakes on it. Use a hand magnifying lens to observe the flakes. What color are the snowflakes? Actually, the snowflakes are as clear as glass, but they reflect light in such a way that they appear to be white. Do the snowflakes have different shapes? Try to draw the basic shape of each snowflake on a sheet of paper? How many points does the snowflake have? Snow usually appears as tiny six-sided crystals, but some flakes may have broken as they fell from the sky.

Measure Snowfall

How much snow falls where you live during a week, a month, or all winter? You can find out by measuring the amount of snowfall with this simple snow gauge. Tape a ruler inside a five-quart (4.75l) ice cream pail. Use a waterproof tape (like Mylar™ tape) and place the ruler so the 1" (2.5 cm) mark is near the bottom. Place the pail in an open area where it is not protected by trees, roofs, or wires. After each snowfall, check the pail and record the amount of snow that fell into the pail. Empty the pail and place it in the same spot until the next snowfall. You might like to keep a chart in your classroom to show how much snow has fallen so far this year. Use different colored markers to indicate snowfalls, if you wish. Young children may need help reading a ruler, and you may wish to record only approximate amounts (to the nearest quarter inch [.625 cm]).

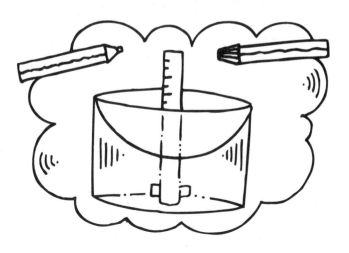

Snow Gallery

Tie a long rope between several trees about 6" (15 cm) above the children's eye level. Then give each child a 9" x 13" (22.5 x 32.5 cm) cardboard frame and two clip-type clothespins. Show the children how to use the frame to create framed pictures of nature. Have each child walk along the roped area and search for something he or she feels would make an interesting picture for his or her frame; then instruct the child to clip the frame to the rope to create the picture. When the picture gallery is complete, take a tour and view the pictures. (Tell the kids to stand about two feet [60 cm] away from each frame.) Invite each child to explain his or her snow picture to the group.

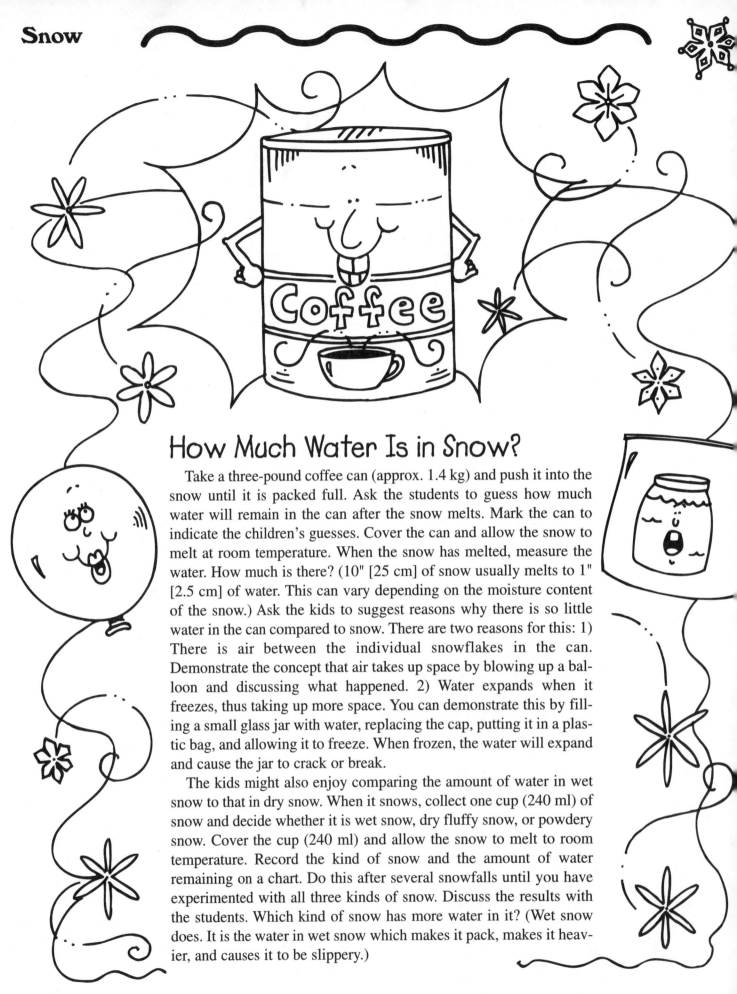

How Much Water Is in Snow?

Take a three-pound coffee can (approx. 1.4 kg) and push it into the snow until it is packed full. Ask the students to guess how much water will remain in the can after the snow melts. Mark the can to indicate the children's guesses. Cover the can and allow the snow to melt at room temperature. When the snow has melted, measure the water. How much is there? (10" [25 cm] of snow usually melts to 1" [2.5 cm] of water. This can vary depending on the moisture content of the snow.) Ask the kids to suggest reasons why there is so little water in the can compared to snow. There are two reasons for this: 1) There is air between the individual snowflakes in the can. Demonstrate the concept that air takes up space by blowing up a balloon and discussing what happened. 2) Water expands when it freezes, thus taking up more space. You can demonstrate this by filling a small glass jar with water, replacing the cap, putting it in a plastic bag, and allowing it to freeze. When frozen, the water will expand and cause the jar to crack or break.

The kids might also enjoy comparing the amount of water in wet snow to that in dry snow. When it snows, collect one cup (240 ml) of snow and decide whether it is wet snow, dry fluffy snow, or powdery snow. Cover the cup (240 ml) and allow the snow to melt to room temperature. Record the kind of snow and the amount of water remaining on a chart. Do this after several snowfalls until you have experimented with all three kinds of snow. Discuss the results with the students. Which kind of snow has more water in it? (Wet snow does. It is the water in wet snow which makes it pack, makes it heavier, and causes it to be slippery.)

Secret Circle

Have all the students stand in a circle in the snow. Each child is to walk no more than 10 steps out from the circle until she sees something interesting. The child then draws an arrow pointing toward her discovery. (This can be a snow formation, a nest in a tree, even an interesting shadow on the snow.) The child then retraces her steps back to the circle. When all the kids are back in the circle, have them move around the circle until all are about two or three places to the right of their starting points. Have each child follow someone else's footsteps and try to find that person's secret discovery. Ask the kids to return to the circle and talk about what each saw.

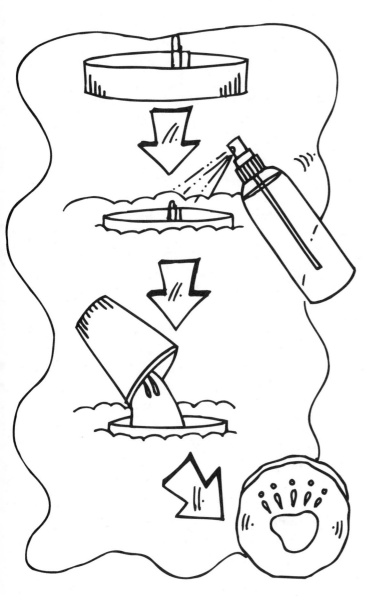

Collecting Tracks

The best time to collect animal tracks is early in the morning on a cold day. Some kids might like to collect animal tracks to bring to school. (Very young children would need help from an older brother or sister or parent.) One method students can use to collect tracks is the plaster-cast method.

1. Make a paper collar from heavy paper or tagboard and a paper clip. The collar should be just a little larger than the track itself. Place the collar over the track and push it into the snow to secure it.

2. Lightly spray the print with very cold water. This will freeze while you are preparing the plaster and make it easier to get a good, clear print.

3. Fill a paper cup halfway with plaster of Paris. Then slowly add water while you stir with a stick. Add only enough water so the plaster becomes thick but still will run slowly.

4. Tap the cup on a rock or the ground five or six times to remove any air bubbles. Then pour the plaster into the track. Wait about 20 minutes for the cast to harden. Remove the print from the snow.

5. See if you can find out what animal made this track.

Snow Writer

Sometimes the tracks in the snow can tell stories. Show the kids the track story below, and ask them to write a story describing what happened. Kids who cannot write yet could dictate the story to an aide or an older child. The animals in the story are a bird, rabbit, dog, and cat.

Children might also enjoy creating their own track stories for their classmates to solve.

Find pictures of other kinds of tracks in the snow, and have the kids explain what happened in each and what made the tracks. Be sure to show enough of the picture to provide some clues. Some possibilities are snowmobile tracks all over a field; various kinds of tire tracks, such as truck tire, tractor tire, snow tire, bicycle tire, and ski or toboggan tracks.

Measure Ground Cover

Does the same amount of snow fall in different places? Try measuring the snow depth at various places around your school. Give each child a ruler and a piece of masking tape. You might wish to mark the 1" (2.5 cm) end of the ruler with marker. Have each student choose a different spot at which to measure the snow depth. Some possibilities are under a tree with no leaves, under a conifer tree, on opposite sides of the same tree, next to the building, in the middle of the school yard, and so on. Instruct each child to place the 1" (2.5 cm) end of the ruler into the snow, pushing it down as far as it will go, and then place the piece of tape on the ruler at the point where it sticks out of the snow. (If you've had a great deal of snow accumulation, you may prefer to use yardsticks instead of rulers.)

Back in the classroom, help the children make a bar graph indicating approximate snow depth in various spots. Where was the snow the deepest? Where did you find the least snow? Why was there less snow under the tree? Why was there more snow on the north side of the building? Help the kids to see that protection from the storm and the direction from which the storm came make a difference.

Inches (cm)	1	2	3	4	5	6	7	8
Under leafless tree								
Under conifer tree								
North side of school								
East side of school								
South side of tree								

Salt and Snow

Ask the kids why people put salt on their sidewalks and why road crews spread rock salt on the highways during the winter. Accept all logical responses. Go outside and collect a container of snow. Take the temperature of the snow. Then add a tablespoon (15 ml) of salt and take the temperature again. Do this several times. What happens to the temperature of the snow? What happens to the snow itself? What happens when salt is spread on roads and sidewalks after it snows?

Color and Melting Snow

Try this experiment on a calm, sunny winter day. Invite each child to choose a different colored sheet of construction paper (including white and black). Have the students place the sheets of paper near each other on the snow in a sunny spot. Ask the kids to guess which color will melt the snow the fastest. After a couple of hours, have the kids check to see where the snow melted the most. Under which colors did the snow melt the quickest? Why? Which colors of paper feel warmer? Darker colors absorb more heat from the sun than lighter colors and cause the snow to melt faster.

Snow Blanket

In regions where the weather is very cold during the winter months, snow is very important. Snow cover on the ground actually works like a blanket and keeps the ground beneath it warmer than the air above it. Air that is moving cools quickly. The air under a blanket of snow does not move so it stays warmer. Even during the winter, there is always warm air rising from the Earth, and snow prevents the air from escaping and mixing with the cold outer air.

On a cold, cloudy winter day, take the kids outside to test the temperature at various levels in a snowdrift. Using regular home thermometers, place one about 1" (2.5 cm) down in the top of a drift, one down into the middle of the drift, and one into the drift at ground level. Leave the thermometers in the drift for a few minutes. Meanwhile, ask the kids where they would burrow into this snowdrift if they were small animals who wanted to stay warm. Remove the thermometers and show the children the temperature at each level.

Have the students speculate how this blanket of snow protects plants and animals. It is the alternate freezing and thawing that kills many plants and insects. Snow keeps the ground temperatures more even so the plants do not freeze and prevents them from being ripped from the ground by wind. Animals that have no burrows under the ground can make nests deep under the snow and stay warm. Ask the kids to name an animal that always makes its home under the snow. (polar bear)

Snow Sculptures

Take advantage of a fresh snowfall to foster environmental awareness among your students. Snow sculptures and the two activities that follow are best suited for use in a wooded area or park.

Nature is a fantastic artist. She waves her snowy wand and transforms the woods into a veritable fairy land complete with fascinating figures never seen before. Take your students to a wooded area or park and look for snow sculptures. Point out a few to your class, and then have the kids search for interesting snow sculptures of their own. When each child has found one that appeals to him, give the children tagboard and markers to create signs. Each child is to think of a name for his sculpture, print it on the tagboard and place the sign near the sculpture. When all the signs are in place, hold a snow sculpture exhibition.

If the snow packs easily, kids might enjoy creating a snowbird or other animal that would fit in with the natural sculptures they found.

Icestimation

Use snow and ice to provide experiences estimating, weighing, and measuring. Fill empty milk cartons with water and freeze several days ahead. Use the frozen ice blocks for the following activities.

1. Peel the paper from the ice block and run warm water over the block. The ice should begin to crack slightly. Set the ice block in a pie pan and gently make several small holes in the top of the ice using a warm ice pick. Drop several drops of food coloring in the holes and set the ice block in the sun. Have students guess how long it will take the blocks to melt. Check on the block several times throughout the day and watch as the colors mix and make other colors.

2. Peel the paper from an ice block and have children take turns holding the block and estimating how much the block weighs. Record their estimations. Weigh the block and record the weight in a secret place until the end of the day. Now ask students to estimate the amount of time it will take the ice to melt. Record your starting time on the board and keep track by half hour increments. At the end of the day, announce the correct weight and melting time and reward the closest estimations with an "ice treat."

3. Perimeter estimation can be done with string. Each child is given an opportunity to look at one of the blocks and then cut a piece of string he or she thinks will fit around the block. Measure the perimeter as a group; cut the correct length of string and have students compare their strings to the correct measurement.

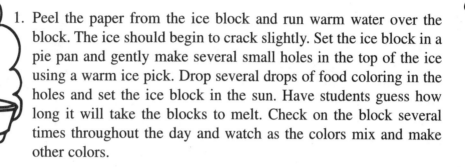

Winter Weather

Weather

Rain, rain, go away,
Come again another day.

It's raining; it's pouring;
The old man is snoring;
He got into bed
And bumped his head
And couldn't get up in the morning.

Although precipitation may be the bane of every outdoorsy child, it plays an important role in our weather cycle. The collision of a warm air mass with a cold air mass will cause the moisture in the air to fall as rain or snow. You can demonstrate this phenomenon for your students with a foil pan and an electric kettle. Heat some water in the kettle until steam is visible. Then fill the pan with cold water and hold it carefully over the steam. The meeting of the hot and the cold will cause droplets to form on the bottom of the pan.

If all the world was apple pie
And all the sea was ink,
And all the trees were bread and cheese,
What would we have to drink?

A fitting complement to this delicious poem is Judith Barrett's book *Cloudy with a Chance of Meatballs* (Atheneum, 1978), a grandfather's silly tale of a town exposed to edible weather. The people are content to base their meals on the provisions of the precipitation until a freaky front forces everyone to flee to a land where people engage in a more traditional way of eating.

36

Daily Weather Board

Tell children that depending on what part of the country we live in, we experience different kinds of weather.

Find pictures of children dressed in the following ways: snowsuits or heavy winter clothing, sweaters or light-weight jogging clothes, swimsuits, and raincoats and umbrellas. Display these pictures on a bulletin board. Ask the children to look at the types of clothing these children are wearing. Say, "Can you tell me something about the winters where these children live by looking at their clothing?"

After you make up a short paragraph about each picture, talk with the children about the climate where you live. Ask, "Which picture is more like the winter weather we have?"

Nature's Snow Cream

Show a picture of maple trees being tapped for maple syrup. Explain the process. Serve each child a small bowl of vanilla ice cream topped with maple syrup.

Daily Weather Board

Provide discarded magazines and catalogs and blunt scissors for each child. Help children select a picture of a boy or girl. Paste on cardboard and laminate or cover with clear Con-Tact™ paper. Glue a small piece of felt to the back of each. Use on a flannelboard in the following way:

1. Display the child's representation on the weather board when they are the Leader for the Day.
2. Place all students' pictures on the board accompanied by the correct weather symbol. Encourage creative questions by asking, "Today our weather symbol shows snow. What could our class do on a snowy day?" (Measure the snow, make angels in the snow, or follow tracks.) "What could we learn by being outside on a sunny day?" (Learn about shadows, how long it takes an ice cube to melt in the sun, or time of day the sun sets.)

Winter Song

Use body movement and sing to the tune of "Here We Go 'Round the Mulberry Bush."

1. This is the way I make a snowball,
   (Pretend to pick up snow and shape into a ball.)
   Make a snowball, make a snowball.
   This is the way I make a snowball,
   So early in the morning.

2. This is the way I build a snowman . . .
   (Start low and build tall.)

3. This is the way Mr. Sun melts it down . . .
   when he comes out to stay.
   (Children slowly fall to the floor.)

Winter Snack

Take a few minutes before snack time to talk about the importance of good nutrition for growing bodies. Mention that food is the fuel our bodies need to run, like a car needs gas. Create a chart showing the following directions for making a snack. Read through, pointing out each word.

1 cup (240 ml)   warm milk

2 teaspoons (10 ml)   chocolate mix

Stir.   Add 1 peppermint stick.

Assist younger children in pouring milk
into individual cups.

Winter Vocabulary

Call out and write the words below on the chalk board.

Encourage children to dictate a story about winter weather. Underline these words. Read several times during the day. Older children may be able to read by themselves. Allow time for illustrating the story.

cold	temperature	long nights
blanket	heavy coat	ice
snow	animal tracks	wind
hot soup	mittens	cap
hill	sled	

Tracks in the Snow

Take a nature walk on a snowy day. Look for tracks made by people, animals, and birds. Ask, "Can you tell how many animals were in this group? What direction are the tracks heading? Are all the bird tracks the same? If not, how are they different?"

Variations of Weather

Discuss how winter weather varies in different sections of the country. Some children live where the weather is mild. Others in rainy areas. Winter lasts longer further north. What is winter like where you live? Ask, "Would you like to trade places with a child who lives where the winter is different? Why or why not?"

Winter Cards

Make a card to send to a friend using blue construction paper, and white, thick poster paint. Place the eraser end of a pencil in the white paint and press on the paper. Allow the child to make his or her creative design. Let dry and fold in half. Give to a parent, grandparent, or friend.

Snow Under a Microscope

Place snowflakes on slides and put under a microscope. Talk about the different shapes. Allow time for drawing snowflakes.

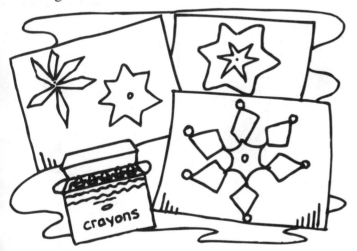

Winter Clothing

Cut a long strip of butcher paper and hang on the wall. Write *Clothes for Rainy Weather* on one half and *Clothes for Ice and Snow* on the other. Use discarded magazines and catalogs to find pictures of children dressed in clothes for rainy weather and those for ice and snow. Paste in the correct sections.

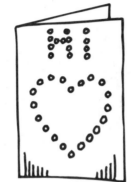

Snow Gauge

Measure the amount of snow or rain that falls. Make a container from the bottom half of a clear plastic soda bottle. Tape a ruler to the side or hold the ruler secure and mark off the inches (centimeters) with a permanent felt-tip marker. Another way is to stand a yardstick up in your yard. However, this is less reliable because of snowdrifts. You may want to compare your amount with the forecast or amount given by the newspaper or television.

References

Baldwin, Barbara. *Celebrate the Seasons.* Monkey Sisters, 1983.

Bauman, Toni, and June Zinkgraf. *Winter Wonders.* Good Apple, 1978.

Casey, Patricia. *Winter Days.* Putnam Publishing Group, 1984.

Cosgrove, Margaret. *It's Snowing!* Dodd, 1980.

Marcus, Elizabeth. *Our Wonderful Seasons.* Troll Associates, 1983.

Markle, Sandra. *Exploring Winter.* Atheneum, 1984.

Moncure, Jane. *Step into Winter: A New Season.* Childrens Press, 1990.

Webster, David. *Exploring Nature Around the Year: Winter.* Julian Messner, 1989.

Williams, Terry T., and Ted Major. *The Secret Language of Snow.* Pantheon, 1984.

Wilson, Ron. *Things to See and Do in Winter.* Young Library, 1986.

Animal Tracks

In the winter, animals leave their "signatures" in the snow in the form of tracks. Animals make tracks when they walk, run, and hop. Have you seen these tracks in the snow? Have you seen these tracks after a rain or when the ground is muddy? Match these "signatures" in the snow with the animals that made them. Write the correct number in each box.

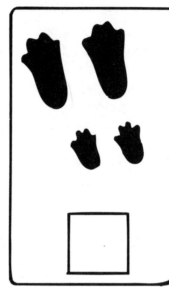
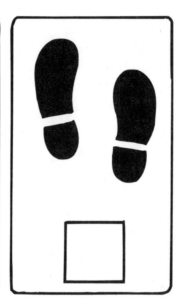
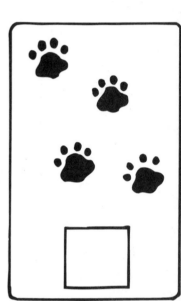

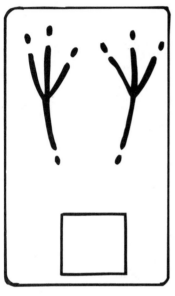

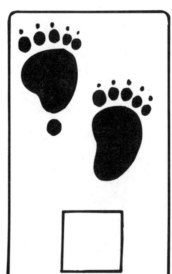
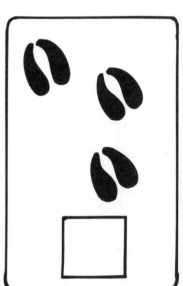

1. dog	5. cat
2. bear	6. bird
3. deer	7. squirrel
4. rabbit	8. human

Answers:
1st row: 6, 4, 8, 5
2nd row: 7, 1, 2, 3

Reproducible

© Fearon Teacher Aids FE7951

Hidden Picture

Cold weather affects animals, birds, and fish in different ways. They may grow warmer coats, migrate (travel to a warmer climate), or hibernate (curl up and sleep for most of the winter). See how many animals you can find hidden in this picture. Look for a snake, squirrel, bear, fish, bird, turtle, rabbit, and frog.

Reproducible

Weather Forecasters

People who study the weather and report the information to us are weather forecasters. Their occupation is listed with others in communications and media. Some other occupations in this category include actor, camera operator, composer, light technician, motion-picture projectionist, reporter, set painter, sportscaster, telephone operator, and newscaster.

What Do Weather Forecasters Do All Day?

Weather forecasters have many responsibilities. They keep track of weather conditions throughout the country using radar and satellites. One of their most important jobs is to determine dangerous weather conditions and warn people to get ready for storms. In addition, they tell farmers the weather which influences when and how they plant, water, or harvest their crops. Weather information comes to the weather forecaster in many ways. It comes from radar, satellites, Teletype™ (a type of computer), phone calls, eyewitnesses, and two-way radios.

Weather forecasters can be regularly seen or heard on television or radio during most news program. They can be seen or heard during emergency situations at anytime.

Tools for the Weather

What does a weather forecaster use when presenting the weather? Allow the children to view a segment of the weather report taped from a local broadcast. Have them list all the things that they see on the screen that the weather forecaster uses. Post these words and pictures on a large television screen with *Weather Forecaster* written at the top.

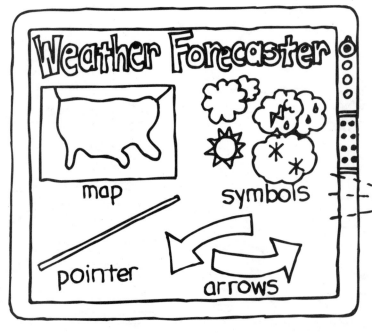

The Weather Forecast

Make a large United States map the children can record the weather on each day. Copy and cut out several of the weather symbols shown here for the children to place on the map. Bring in the daily weather maps from the local newspaper or assign the responsibility to a child. Transfer the information from the weather map to the large class map.

patterns

What Is the Weather?

Have children check the weather for five days and tell in their own words what it looks like outside. Use the thermometers on page 44 to record the temperature at a given time each day for one week. If you have time, post thermometers in sequence all around the room. Do this for a month or even the entire year. Record the temperature twice a day for morning and afternoon sessions, keeping the morning temperatures at the bottom and the afternoon temperatures above them. Have children tell you about the differences in morning and afternoon temperatures. At the end of the week, invite the children to tell you about the weather for the week. Has it gotten warmer? Is it getting colder? How do they know? What do they think will happen next? Why?

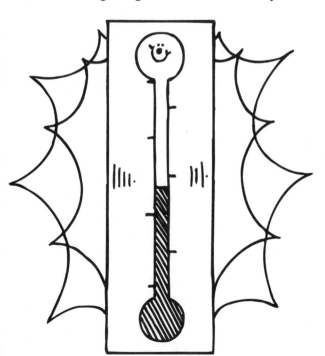

Children's Books

Branley, F.M. *Tornado Alert*. Harper & Row, 1988.
  A *Let's Read and Find Out Book* with pictures and facts about tornadoes. Another in the series is *Hurricane Watch*.
Martin, C. *I Can Be a Weather Forecaster*. Childrens Press, 1987.
  Tools and equipment of weather forecasting are shown with male and female forecasters of various races.
Wiesner, D. *Hurricane*. Clarion Books, 1990.

Reproducible

Name _____

This Week's Temperatures

On each thermometer record the temperature in red at _____.
(insert time)

Then record the temperature at _____ in blue.
(insert time)

90	90	90	90	90
80	80	80	80	80
70	70	70	70	70
60	60	60	60	60
50	50	50	50	50
40	40	40	40	40
40	40	40	40	40
20	20	20	20	20

44

Reproducible

Take-Home Weather Chart

Record the weather during a seven-day period. Encourage parents to help their child select the appropriate symbol. The child may draw his or her own version of the weather or copy the patterns.

Rain	Sun	Fog	Clouds
		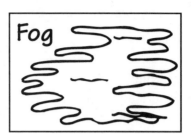	

Snow	Wind	Sunday
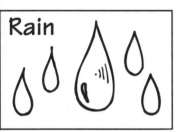		

Monday	Tuesday	Wednesday
Thursday	Friday	Saturday

Trees

Anytime of the year is a good time to study trees. In many areas of the country, the leaves on some trees change colors starting in mid-September and continuing through late October and early November. In the Deep South the trees might stay green all year.

As part of an environmental study, children can plant trees from seeds and watch them change over time. Children certainly gain joy as they watch their seeds sprout, their seedlings grow, and their trees gain height.

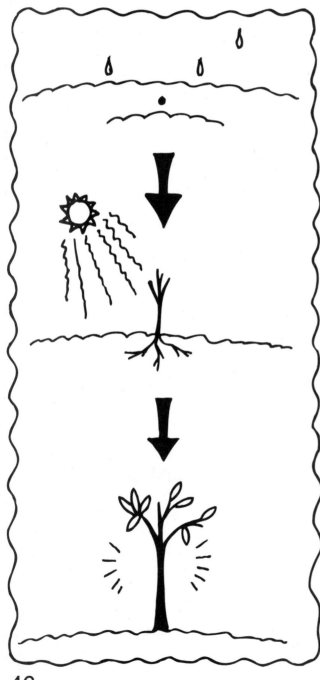

Choose a Tree

Take a tree walk on your playground or in your neighborhood. Invite each child to choose one tree to be considered his or her "own." Make sure each child is able to easily define its characteristics and remember which one is "his or hers." Stop at each tree and describe its shape, the texture of the bark, the shape of the leaves, its height, and so on. You might also number the trees and write down the characteristics yourself so you can remember which trees are which.

When the children get back to the room, have them try to find someone else who has chosen the same tree they have. If they find someone, they go as a pair to find others who have chosen the same tree.

When all children are grouped, ask the children to sit in line to show which tree they chose. Count the number in each group to see which tree was chosen the most times, the least, and so on. Graph the results on a class graph. (A giant tarp divided into 1' [30 cm] squares is great for a class graph. Use various shapes of trees similar to the ones on your walk to mark the spots.)

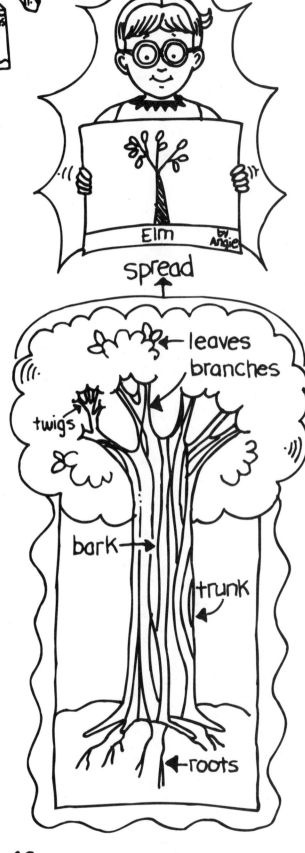

My Tree

After children have spent time verbally describing their trees, have them return to their trees with drawing supplies: pencils, paper, lapboards, crayons, and erasers.

Invite the children to choose a spot near the trees and draw "their" trees with pencil and then color them.

Label the tree with its actual name at the bottom of the page. Use all of the children's trees for a bulletin board called, "Look What's in Our Neighborhood!"

Tree Word Bank

Children need direct experiences to develop new vocabulary. After their trip to describe the trees and the trip to draw the trees, cut out a giant 3' (90 cm) high tree from white paper.

Solicit words the children know that describe trees. These might include: *bark, leaves, branches, twigs, roots, trunk, spread,* and so on. As you record their responses, label the parts of the tree with the terms used.

Leaf Collecting

When the leaves are falling off the trees or when the trees are being trimmed back, let the children collect leaves from the trees. Make sure that you have at least one leaf per child. These are best used if they are preserved in some way. You may press them, iron them between two sheets of waxed paper, or laminate them.

Ask the children to put all their leaves together. Have the children sort them by shape, size, and color.

Naming Leaves

After activities have been completed, ask the children to pick one leaf of each kind. Provide 8 1/2" x 11" (21.3 cm x 27.5 cm) pieces of paper for each leaf. Fold the paper in half, glue the leaf to one side of the paper, and write the name of the tree from which it came on the other half. Older children can describe the tree further in writing.

I Can Be as Tall as a Tree

Use the children as outlines for trees. Have the children lie on pieces of butcher paper and trace around them. Use their bodies as the trunks of the trees. Have the children make the leaves.

- Make prints from precut sponges and tempera paint.
- Glue on real leaves.
- Make leaf rubbings. Cut out the leaf rubbings and glue them to the top of the tree.
- Place a leaf under the top of the tree. Make 30 to 40 rubbings of this leaf at various places at the top of the tree.

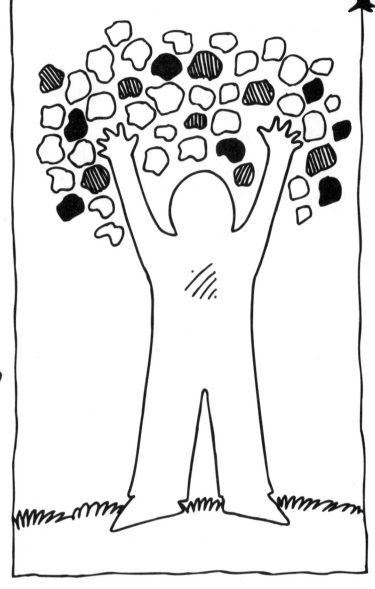

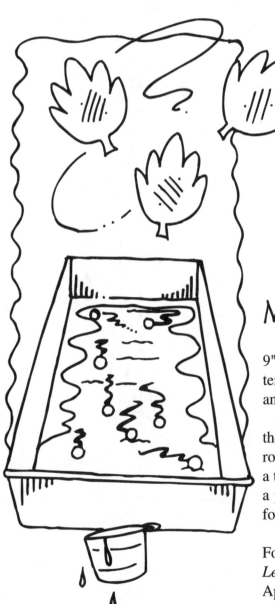

Mixing Fall Colors

Place 1/2 cup (120 ml) of yellow tempera paint in the bottom of a 9" x 12" (22.5 cm x 30 cm) cake pan. Place several marbles in red tempera. Let the children place the red marble in the yellow paint and tip the pan to mix new colors.

Place precut maple-leaf shapes in the paint to print the colors on the leaves. Use these leaves for the top of a maple tree in the classroom. Each child will make one leaf for the class tree and several for a tree of his or her own to take home. The trunk of the tree could be a piece of brown construction paper or a brown print of his or her forearm.

For further study about trees, see the book, *Centers for Early Learners Throughout the Year* (GA1334) by Jeri A. Carroll, Good Apple, 1991.

What Does a Tree Give Us?

In each box draw a picture of something that trees give us. After you draw the picture, write words that tell us about your picture.

Leaves

Fall is the perfect time to collect leaves. Children can gather them from the trees in the area and from the ground. They can mail them to friends in other parts of the country, solicit them from their friends, exchange them, mount them, label them, chart them, and graph them.

Collect leaves weekly. Save between two sheets of clear Con-Tact™ paper. Cut into leaf shapes. Display on bulletin board.

Collect leaves. Laminate and cut around them. Sort into containers. Use on a tree board. Use for counting. Or, graph the collection.

Choose a special leaf. Put leaf into a dish of tempera paint. Lift out. Blot between two pieces of paper several times. Label the parts of the leaf.

Collect leaves. Trace around each leaf that is different. Sort into leaf piles.

Gather leaves. Press between pages of a heavy book. Place under piece of paper. Run crayon lengthwise across paper to make a leaf rubbing.

Have each child make a bark rubbing from a tree trunk with a brown crayon on a piece of 6" x 18" (15 cm x 45 cm) white paper. Glue each rubbing to long butcher paper. Glue on collected leaves.

Pumpkin Patch

Pumpkins, Melons, and Other Fruits

Pumpkins belong to the same family of plants as squash. Some squash that kids might recognize are acorn, butternut, habbard, zucchini, white bush scallop, and crookneck. Ask the kids to suggest some ways pumpkins, squash, and melons are alike. (They grow on trailing vines close to the ground; have outer shells, seeds, and edible pulp inside; contain a great deal of water; and are often hollow.)

Cut out pictures of various pumpkins, squash, melons, and other fruits from a seed catalog. Glue the pictures on individual index cards. Have the kids classify the fruits by distinguishing characteristics: those that have thick, fairly hard outer shells; those with thin or soft skins; those which grow on trailing vines and those which don't; or any other classification that would separate the pumpkins, squash, and melons from other fruits.

Recognizing Pumpkins

The kids might enjoy comparing pumpkins to other kinds of squash. Have them note the similarities and differences in shape, size, color, and weight of each. (Use a scale to weigh the pumpkin and squash.) Cut them open and compare the thickness of the outer shells, the inner pulp, the size and arrangement of the seeds, and the smells and tastes. Kids might also enjoy opening the seeds to see the tiny embryos inside. After the children have had an opportunity to compare the pumpkin and squash, see if they can identify the pumpkin among the others by using their various senses. Blindfold a child and have him or her use his or her sense of touch to find the pumpkin among the other squash. A small pumpkin and an acorn squash seem fairly similar to the touch. Can the child recognize pieces of pumpkin by taste and smell in comparison to other squash pieces?

Grow a Pumpkin Plant

Students can germinate some pumpkin seeds of their own in a classroom. If this is done in the spring, the young seedlings can be planted outside to produce pumpkins in the fall. Try germinating a few seeds between layers of damp paper towels so that the children can see what a sprouting seed looks like. Since most seeds are usually planted deep in the ground, the kids have probably never seen this happen.

Other pumpkin seeds can be planted in empty milk cartons. Soak some of the seeds in lukewarm water for a day. Poke holes in the bottoms of half-gallon (1.9 l) milk cartons. Fill the cartons with potting soil to 11/2" (3.75 cm) from the top. Put two seeds in each carton and cover with 1" (2.5 cm) of soil. (Plant soaked seeds in one carton and unsoaked seeds in another.) Press lightly on the soil. Pour one cup (240 ml) of water down the inside edge of the carton so as not to disturb the seeds. Then sprinkle some water on top of the soil. Cover each carton with plastic wrap and place in a warm place. Have the kids keep track of which seeds germinate first. Soaked seeds will usually sprout in about five days; unsoaked seeds take seven to ten days to germinate. Ask the kids to suggest the reasons that some seeds sprouted more quickly.

When the seeds have sprouted, remove the plastic wrap and put the cartons in a sunny spot. In about a week, cut off the smaller of the plants. Water every other day with one cup (240 ml) of water for about four weeks before planting outside.

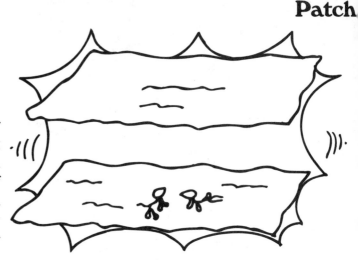

Food Value of Pumpkins

There are two groups of pumpkins: the yellow (straw-colored) cheese pumpkin (which is used for commercially canned pumpkin) and the big orange stock pumpkin (which is used for carving jack-o'-lanterns and as food for livestock). As a food source, pumpkins are a fair source of energy. They are about 90% water but are rich in phosphorus, calcium, iron, vitamins A and B, and are a fair source of vitamin C. Discuss each vitamin and nutrient and how it benefits human health.

If kids carve jack-o'-lanterns, recycle some of the seeds for a healthy snack. Wash the seeds under cold water to remove the stringy material. Dry the seeds between paper towels. Mix 11/2 tablespoons (22.5 ml) vegetable oil, 1 teaspoon (5 ml) salt, and 2 cups (470 ml) pumpkin seeds in a bowl. Spread the seeds in a single layer on a cookie sheet. Roast the seeds in a preheated 350^{0}F oven until lightly brown and crispy. Stir the seeds occasionally. Depending on the moisture content of the seeds, it will take 30 minutes to one hour to roast. Dry the seeds on a paper towel and store in a covered container.

While kids nibble on the warm seeds, share a pumpkin tale with them. *The Pumpkin People* by David and Maggie Cavagnaro (Sierra Club Books/Charles Scribner's Sons, 1979) is a natural adventure story in which a young boy and his family plant pumpkin and squash seeds and later carve the pumpkins and squash into jack-o'-lanterns with unique personalities as a part of their harvest celebration. The book traces the birth, growth, death, and rebirth of the pumpkin and squash plants.

Gardens from Invisible Seeds

Wait! Don't throw away that jack-o'-lantern yet. Keep it in your room and let your students discover a special garden that grows from invisible seeds.

Several days after Halloween (or any other time), help your students use a magnifying glass to examine the white fuzzy mold growing in the pumpkin. Ask your class where they think these tiny plants came from.

The "plants" they discovered inside the pumpkin are rhizopus (rise-uh-puss), a fungus or mold that grows on things that contain starch and sugar. Molds don't develop from seeds but grow from airborne cells called *spores*. These spores are almost everywhere and will appear when conditions are right for growth.

The pumpkin garden will soon begin to smell as the mold really starts to grow. You will have to get rid of the pumpkin garden, but you can help your students start their own little garden by collecting invisible seeds and planting them in a special way.

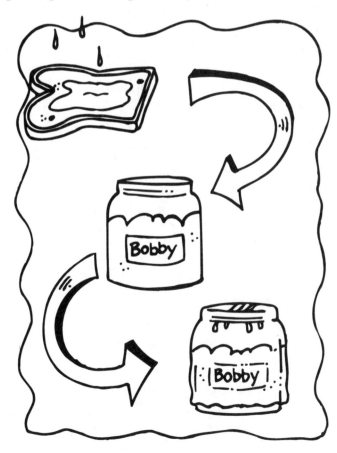

Garden 1

Materials

one baby food jar with lid per child, small pieces of white bread for each child, masking tape, and pen to label jars

Directions

Label the jars with one child's name on each. Have the children place the bread inside the jars. Sprinkle water on the bread until it is thoroughly moistened. Pour off any excess water. Leave the soggy bread open to the air at room temperature for about one hour. This will give the bread enough time to gather spores from the air.

Cover the jars with plastic wrap and set the jars in a dark warm place where they won't be disturbed. Save the jar lids for the children to use when they take their "gardens" home.

Garden 2

Materials

one baby food jar with lid per child, tomato soup (uncooked), masking tape, and pen to label jars

Directions

Label the jars with one child's name on each. Pour one tablespoon (15 ml) of soup in each jar. Let each child select one of the methods below to collect spores to plant in the soup:

- sprinkle dirt on the soup
- sprinkle bread crumbs on the soup
- rub finger across the floor and stick that finger in the soup

After planting the spores, label each jar with the method of planting used. Cover the jars with plastic wrap and put them in a warm, dark place.

Within a week the gardens should be growing. Rhizopus and possibly blue-green penicillium, black mucor, or skinny thread-like aspergillus should appear. You will need to examine your soup or bread with a magnifying glass to discover the differences in the molds. Rhizopus will also grow little black spots like a knob at the tip. These black spots are spore cases. When they are moved or when they dry out, they will release thousands of spores. You can try to touch the spore cases with a toothpick and then look at them with a magnifying glass.

To extend this activity, you might encourage scientific reasoning by setting up this control group experiment.

Question: Will mold grow in cold places?
Procedure: Label four baby food jars—two with *cold/dark* and two with *warm/dark.*

Have children place a small piece of the same kind of bread in each jar. Wet the bread with the same amount of water for each piece. Drain the excess water and leave the jars open for one hour. Cover the jars and place two of the jars in the refrigerator and two in a warm, dark place.

Encourage the children to predict in which jars rhizopus will appear first. Write down the predictions. Help your students understand why it was important for them to do exactly the same thing with each jar. (Penicillium may grow in the cold jars.) Compare the gardens and check the predictions.

Students can cover their gardens with lids and take them home to share.

Note: Children who have known allergies to mold and dust should not be allowed to touch the mold. Be sure the students wash their hands after working with their gardens.

Dirt

Dirty Collection

Collect dirt of different colors and textures. Ask the children to describe the location where the soil was found (under trees, by a creek, near many rocks, and so on). Allow children to feel the various soils and experiment with their textures by shaping them. Is the soil sticky, sandy, dry? Use a magnifying glass to discover if there are any insects, worm eggs, or leaf particles in the soil. Ask the children to find a crayon color that matches each soil sample and draw a picture with that color.

Soil Recipe

Have children examine soil they have scooped from under a bush. Guide them to discover ingredients in the soil that came from the bush. Discuss how soil is made from organic materials, weather, and animal matter. Ask the children to describe the smell of the soil. Put the soils into glass jars. Leave 3" (7.5 cm) of space at the top of the jar. Slowly pour water into the jar of soil. Bubbles will percolate up through the soil into the water. Ask, "What's inside a bubble? Does this mean soil has air in it?" Put the lid on the jar and shake vigorously (have children take turns on this task). Let the water and soil mixture settle and watch how layers of sand, clay, pebbles, and humus form. Discuss and compare contents of each layer. You can try this experiment with a variety of soils.

Water in Soil

Put different types of soil in jars, half full. Cover each sample tightly with a lid. Set the jars in a warm area. Water droplets will soon form on the glass walls of the jars. Ask the children, "Where did the water come from? Why is water needed in the soil? (for plant and animal life, soil conservation) How did the water get there? What would happen if there was not water in the soil?" Try the same experiment with sand.

Dig to China

Show children a globe of the Earth and point out where they live and where China is located. Discuss what would happen if they tried to "dig" to China. Select a loose soil area where children can dig a deep hole (12" [30 cm] or more). Examine the Earth's changes. Discover roots, categorize what is found, discuss color of soil layers, and feel differences in temperature. Fill in the hole again, and discuss why all the dirt does not fit back inside.

Dust to Dust

Scoop up a collection of moist soil and place it in a jar. Have children add a leaf or plant section to a visible area. Cover the jar. Ask children to predict what will happen to the leaf. Guess how long it will take for mold to form on the leaf. Record how long it actually takes. Why is mold needed? (Mold breaks down plants which form the soil.)

Finger Pots

Form a ball of "mud clay." Press thumb into the ball to make a pot. Let it dry.

Balancing Act

Provide different types of soil in small buckets near some scales. Provide a one-cup (240 ml) measure. Have children measure one cup (240 ml) of two different kinds of soil to see which is the heaviest or lightest.

Dirt Dump

Provide children with dump trucks and different sized containers. Let them estimate how many containers full of dirt it will take to fill the dump truck. Try it.

The Bucket Brigade

Place a mound of dirt at one end of the area. Provide a box of containers that can be filled with dirt. Have the children decide how to move the mound of dirt from one end of the area to the other.

Archaeological Dig

Archaeology is the study of old objects, such as buildings, tools, and bones. Archaeologists are scientists that look for and study old objects. Over a million years ago, the first people appeared on Earth. These people grew crops, made tools, built fires, and erected villages. They left behind items, such as coins, statues, tools, houses, ships, jewelry, and tombs. Many objects have been covered by dirt over the years or are beneath the ocean. Archaeologists try to find hidden treasures. They look for clues in books, use photographs, and listen to old stories. Underwater cameras help find ships that have sunk to the bottom of the ocean.

An archaeological dig is a place where old objects might be found. Archaeologists begin by digging holes in the ground around the object. This helps them know how deep they will need to dig. Trenches are dug to find the size of the area. Old objects can easily be broken, so they must be taken from the ground with care. Special tools, such as a little knife or brush, help to remove the objects. Pictures are taken of objects when they are found. Archaeologists try to learn what an object is made of so that they can get an idea of how old it is.

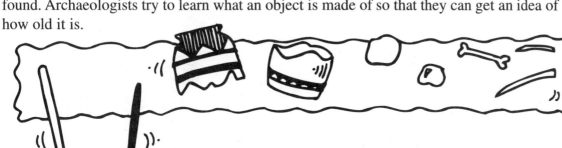

Make Your Own Archaeological Site

Find objects to put into your archaeological site, such as small bones, fossils, broken pottery, and rocks.

Clean a pint-size (470 ml) milk carton.

Fold over the pointed end of the carton and tape it down.

Turn the carton on its side. With scissors, cut the long side off.

Put your objects in the carton.

Pour two parts plaster of Paris in a mixing bowl.

Add one part water. Mix until smooth.

Pour the plaster of Paris in the carton around the objects.

Let it dry. Then remove the carton.

You are now ready to dig. Find brushes and small scraping tools. Have the children remove the objects by carefully scraping and brushing the plaster away.

Birds

Spring Sign

Show the children a picture of a robin. Have them name the colors of a robin. Use a map to show where different birds migrate for the winter months. Robins generally head south, although a few brave ones stay in cold climates throughout the winter. Explain that when robins return, it means spring is near. Have a contest to see which child can spot the first robin to arrive in your immediate area. Have him or her describe when and where it was seen. Have the kids draw pictures of robins.

Spring Bird Hike

Have children walk outdoors to listen and look for signs of birds. Have them describe when a bird was seen and what it was doing. Ask kids to include size, color, and actions, such as hopping, walking, zigzag flight, and posture on tree, as part of the description. Have students then give each bird its own descriptive name. Invite each child to take turns imitating bird movements while others try to name the specific bird being imitated. Watch for birds feeding.

Nesting

Read portions of the book *Bird* by David Burnie (Knopf, 1988). Prior to walking outdoors, discuss where nests should be located for protection against weather, people, and animals. Ask, "What is used to make nests?" Have children look for places outdoors to put their own nests while they collect materials to build them themselves. Try building nests outdoors. A mud or clay nest form provides a sticky surface for the twigs and grass.

Bird Uses

Discuss with children the uses of birds in a natural environment and in the home. Ask the children to tell what birds do outdoors that helps plants and animals. (They eat insects and carry seeds. Some birds are food for other animals, such as coyotes and large rodents.) Discuss how birds are used by people. (People eat their meat and eggs and use their feathers for decorative purposes.) If possible, obtain fertile eggs so the children may observe the hatching process.

Spiders and Bugs

Spiders

Spiders can be found in corners near ceilings, in dark locations, and also outdoors near walls and in gardens. Keep spiders in a large glass container with a screen lid. A bit of water and a few insects will provide food for the spiders if confined over a period of time. Have children count the legs of a spider and its body parts. Try to find the place where silk is emitted for the web.

Spiderwebs

Spiderwebs, when found, are not easily moved, but try using a large piece of paper set behind the web to hold it together as it is removed. If a spider in a web is available for observation, have the kids look at the spider as it leaves its web carrying a dragline for a quick return. Watch the spider make this web. Examine a web with a magnifying glass, and ask the children to describe the web and its purpose (home, place to snare food). Have children pretend to be spiders making webs. Use a ball of yarn and have kids sit in various locations in the room. Give the yarn to one child, and have him or her roll the ball from child to child, trailing the yarn behind, thus creating a web.

Bug Count

Have the students carry a wide-top container with a screen lid and a fine mesh net to capture insects. Insects will be found in shrubs, cracks of tree trunks, on lawns, along walls outdoors, and in gardens. When children have a collection, ask them to count the insects, the number of legs, and the number of body parts. Have the kids name the insects according to their appearance or sound. Tell them to decide if each insect is a flyer, hopper, or crawler, and describe the colors and the sounds of each insect. Follow up with a role play where students imitate a particular insect. Have the other children try to guess which one it is.

Ants

Ants can be found crawling in the lawns or trees, or they can be enticed with a bit of sweet, moist food set onto the ground surface. An anthill (usually near dry, loose soil) is a good location where children can observe the work of ants. Watch how the work is often shared with other ants. Note the size of the item carried and compare it to the size of the ant. Place an ant on a child's arm so he or she can experience the feel of an ant crawling, and observe how the ant does not seem to be affected by the angle in which the arm is held. Examine and count the ant's body parts. Ask, "What do ants do to help the Earth? Are they food for other animals? Which ones?"

Flies

The most likely place to find flies is along window wells. Collect a variety of dead flies and place on a display surface for children to examine. Ask questions regarding size, color, number of wings. Examine flies with a magnifying glass, paying special attention to the large compound eyes. Ask, "What do flies eat? (plants and animal fluids) What animals eat flies? (lizards, birds, fish, spiders) Are flies good for our environment?" (provide food for animals, insects) Be sure children wash their hands after handling dead flies.

Rocks

Water Rock

Have students hike along the creek edge to collect rocks of varying sizes near an in the water. Find a smooth, rounded rock in the creek bed. Ask, "Why is it smooth? Find a rough rock alongside the creek edge. Ask, "What will make it smooth? Wha do rocks do for the creek? (help prevent erosion, provide a surface for plant life or animal eggs) What does water do for the rocks? How do rocks help the animals in an around the creek?" (Rocks can be homes for animals and insects, add minerals to th water, and provide a surface on which animals may walk.)

Rock Home

Locate a large rock (1' [30 cm] circumference or more), making certain the rock has been in one location outdoors for some time. Ask the children to lift up the rock carefully. Under the rock, the surface of the Earth is a micro-community where only certain animals, insects, and plants exist. Ask, "What color are the plants? Why?" (Most plants will be whitish in color due to the lack of sunlight.) Feel the temperature of the rock surface; feel the ground under the rock and beside it. Discuss why it is cooler under the rock. Set the rock back in place.

Rock Walk

As a group, have children collect rocks and pebbles of all sizes. Have them describe each rock: size, color, texture, and where it was found. Ask the children how the rock got to the place where it was found. "What's the purpose of rocks? (Rocks provide homes for insects, add minerals to the soil, and help control erosion.) Do rocks float? Get rusty? Moldy? Dissolve in water?" Experiment to find the answer to each question. "Are rocks alive? What do rocks do for animals? For man?"

Rock Talk

Display rock collections in a line on the floor. Announce a rock description. For example, say, "Find a round rock with pink and gray spots." Ask each child to find a specific rock. Allow time for each child to participate at his or her own speed. Then set each rock in a special location for its category (color, texture). Combine descriptions: gray and smooth or sharp and dark.

Nature Hike

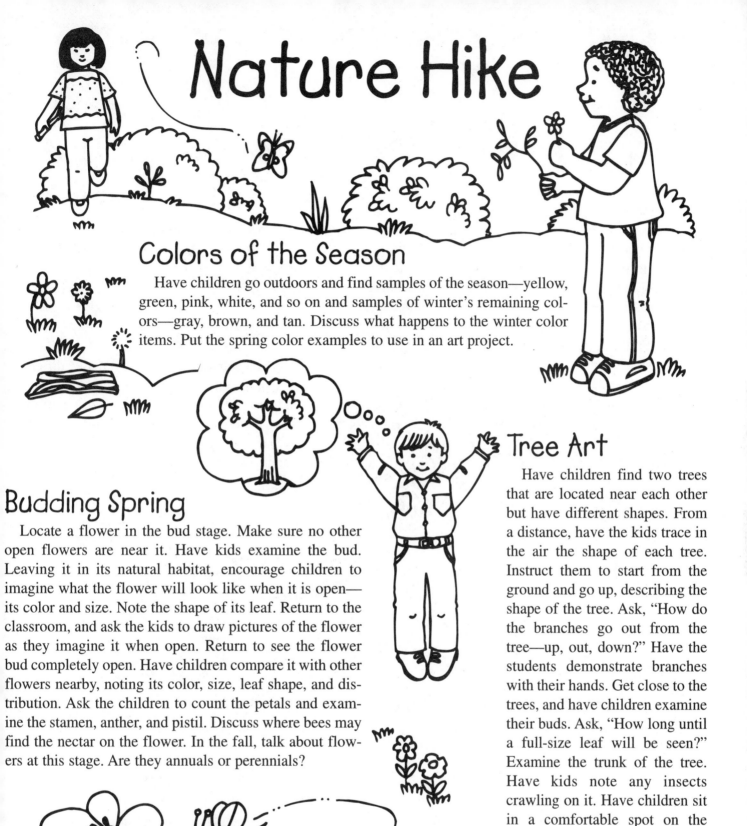

Colors of the Season

Have children go outdoors and find samples of the season—yellow, green, pink, white, and so on and samples of winter's remaining colors—gray, brown, and tan. Discuss what happens to the winter color items. Put the spring color examples to use in an art project.

Budding Spring

Locate a flower in the bud stage. Make sure no other open flowers are near it. Have kids examine the bud. Leaving it in its natural habitat, encourage children to imagine what the flower will look like when it is open—its color and size. Note the shape of its leaf. Return to the classroom, and ask the kids to draw pictures of the flower as they imagine it when open. Return to see the flower bud completely open. Have children compare it with other flowers nearby, noting its color, size, leaf shape, and distribution. Ask the children to count the petals and examine the stamen, anther, and pistil. Discuss where bees may find the nectar on the flower. In the fall, talk about flowers at this stage. Are they annuals or perennials?

Tree Art

Have children find two trees that are located near each other but have different shapes. From a distance, have the kids trace in the air the shape of each tree. Instruct them to start from the ground and go up, describing the shape of the tree. Ask, "How do the branches go out from the tree—up, out, down?" Have the students demonstrate branches with their hands. Get close to the trees, and have children examine their buds. Ask, "How long until a full-size leaf will be seen?" Examine the trunk of the tree. Have kids note any insects crawling on it. Have children sit in a comfortable spot on the grass. With paper and crayon, instruct them to draw the shape of the tree. They can add color to reflect the season.

Lawn Look

Shovel up a cross-section of lawn (about 12" [30 cm] in diameter and 12" [30 cm] deep). Show it to the children, and ask them to follow the roots of individual grass blades. Encourage an understanding of the lawn's purpose by asking a child to uproot a grass plant. Ask, "What would happen to the Earth, other plants, insects, and animals if there were no grass?" "What happens to the grass that is cut? Where does it go? Where is it now? Does it help the soil?" Return the earth and lawn sample to its original location. Have the students water it and later watch to see it continue growing.

Greenfields

Have the children gather as many different shades of green plants as they can find in the school yard. Collect the samples. Instruct the kids to arrange them in color sequences—light to dark green, size sequences—thin to thick, or texture sequences—smooth to rough.

A World of Discovery

Ask the children to make the following observations: Do you see places where grass grows better than it does in others? Why doesn't it grow by the downspout? How does the grass feel to the touch? Why are there rocks or gravel by the downspout? Have children predict what might be found under a stone, a pile of wood, or a tangle of vines. What different materials cover the playground? Discuss the differences between concrete, asphalt, grass, crushed rock, etc. Take a close look at the cracks. Are there little insects in those cracks? Are there plants growing there? Look around the foundations of buildings. Why do plants grow there? Have children collect some of them to take back to the classroom for a closer examination. Are there any animals in the school yards? Why do plants lean away from the building? Is there a fence? Do fences offer plants any advantage? Do fences change living conditions for plants and animals?

Nature's Music

Have kids create a rhythm band using natural objects they collect outdoors. For the rhythm section, use different-sized sticks and rocks with a variety of surfaces and densities, for example, rough and smooth rocks and thick sticks. Place seeds and pebbles in a "shaker" can to create another sound. Conduct rhythm to a favorite class sing-along.

Nature Detective

Collect samples of plants. Give one to each child, and have the child search for a plant that matches this sample. Ask the child to label his or her plant (if the real name has been discussed in class) or give it his or her own descriptive name.

Yard Shapes

The school yard is a good location to discover the differences in size and shape of living plants. Show the children a circle shape and ask them to locate a very large plant that has the shape (a big, full, round tree trunk) and a small example of that shape (a section of a clover leaf). Try finding medium-sized examples of that shape. Repeat this process with various shapes.

Disappearing

Ask the children to describe the colors they see occurring naturally outdoors. Give each child a sample of a color seen outdoors to take home, and ask him or her to dress in a matching camouflage color. Play hide-and-seek. Children will experience how animals hide from predators. Ask, "Why is it necessary for animals and insects to be the same color as their surroundings?" Introduce the word *camouflage*. Do colors of insects or animals change with the seasons? Why? Example: rabbit.

Signs of the Season

Walk outdoors to discover signs of the season. Encourage children to note things they can and can't see and hear or smell: birds and their sounds, color of leaves, absence of leaves, brown and green grass, colder and warmer temperatures. Measure children's shadows and ask, "Are shadows longer or shorter now?" Examine a lawn or tree trunk close up to look for insects. Are there any bugs, why or why not?

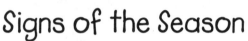

Plant Notes

Mark off areas in 3' (90 cm) squares. Divide the class into groups and assign each group to a square. First have children count the kinds of plants in their square. How many of each were found? Then have the children identify other things found within the square. Finally, have kids sit in a circle and discuss what they have seen. What kinds of soil were found in the various areas? Collect some in a plastic bag. Is there any sand on the playground? Where did it come from?

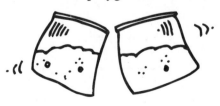